COLLINS GEM
CATS
a mine of information

COLLINS GEM
Chinese
ASTROLOGY
a mine of information

COLLINS GEM
Classic
BOOKS
a mine of information

COLLINS GEM
Classic
FILMS
a mine of information

COLLINS GEM
HORSES
& PONIES
a mine of information

COLLINS GEM
INSECTS
a mine of information

COLLINS GEM
KINGS &
QUEENS
a mine of information

COLLINS GEM
MUSHROOMS
& TOADSTOOLS
a mine of information

COLLINS GEM
SNAKES
a mine of information

D0869206

GEM
OT
...tion

COLLINS GEM
WINE
Guide
a mine of information

COLLINS GEM
WORLD
atlas
a mine of information

COLLINS GEM
YOGA
a mine of information

COLLINS GEM
ZODIAC
Types
a mine of information

COLLINS GEM

SUPERSTITIONS

C. M. Braysher

HarperCollins*Publishers*

C M Braysher is a long-time student of omens, superstitions and folklore.

HarperCollins Publishers
PO Box, Glasgow G4 0NB

First published 1999

Reprint 10 9 8 7 6 5 4 3 2 1 0

ISBN 0 00 472318 X

Printed in Italy by Amadeus S.p.A.

Contents

Introduction

Are you superstitious? Do you wish on shooting stars, avoid walking under ladders or feel apprehensive as Friday the 13th approaches? We all know of the big, popular superstitions, like knocking on wood or crossing your fingers for luck, but most of us would be struggling to remember more than a dozen of them at any time.

Not so in the past – before mass communications and before even literacy was commonplace, people tried to make sense of the harsh, hostile and dangerous world around them by using superstitions. You will see, even from the selection chosen for this book, how these beliefs seeped into every aspect of life. When people could expect to live for just 30 years; when they could expect to be in pain most of the time and outlive half their children; and with their life and health hanging precariously on the outcome of the next harvest, people seized on any omen or portent that might offer a crumb of certainty. Few incidents and objects, even the most trivial, didn't have a superstition or omen attached to them to help predict or control what would happen in their unpredictable world.

In our own age of instant electronic information, when we could never live long enough to take in all the information available to us, superstitious belief seems increasingly a thing of the past. But the popularity of subjects like the paranormal and new-age beliefs also shows that the wheel of belief has turned full circle and even now we still look for the basic, elemental forces that dictate how our lives are governed.

So here is a selection of the innumerable superstitions that used to rule people's lives from the cradle to the grave. You may find them quaint, bizarre and even grotesque, but I hope that every page has something informative and entertaining – I'll keep my fingers crossed!

PEOPLE

Omens and superstitions of basic human experiences, and especially of marriage and death, are so wide-spread that they crop up right across the range of traditional beliefs.

Experiences

BABIES AND BIRTH

When you have one,
You can get up and run.
When you have two,
You can go, too.
When you have three,
Better stay where you be.
When you have four,
You go no more.

The happy burden of parenthood is cele-brated – and warned against – in this old rhyme. Having a child was the most important

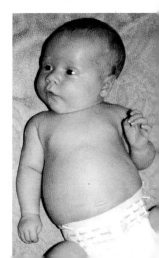

experience in most people's lives and plenty of superstitions reminded them of the weight of their responsibility. They dictated what women should and should not do in pregnancy, how to make sure of their baby's sex, what should be done with the baby when it was born, and how to tell their infant's personality from the moment of its birth. Many of the superstitions were contradictory, and only a neurotic with an exceptional memory could ever hope to carry out all of them. A few are listed here.

DOS AND DON'TS OF PREGNANCY

- don't weigh yourself
- don't look at yourself in a mirror
- eat whatever you crave, or your child will have a physical imprint of the desired food on its body
- a baby carried high will be a girl, low a boy
- to make sure of a girl, put a frying pan under your mattress; for a boy, put a knife there. Or, wear pink for a girl and blue for a boy
- avoid anything ugly or unpleasant, in case it imprints its image on the child
- don't go near a dead body or a grave
- don't knit, sew or spin
- don't swallow an octopus egg while swimming, or you will give birth to an octopus

Newborns After the baby's birth, the rituals really got going.

- a baby born on the stroke of midnight can see ghosts
- a new baby should sneeze to get rid of any evil spirits
- a baby born with a caul (the amniotic membrane) on its body will be lucky; the caul itself was also highly prized
- spitting on a new baby is lucky (but obviously not for the baby)
- a new baby should always be carried up, e.g. stairs, before being brought down
- a baby born with a tooth will be selfish
- a baby born with its hands open will be either careless or generous
- stepping over a crawling baby stunts its growth
- a baby shouldn't be allowed to see its reflection in a mirror until it is a year old
- a baby smiling in its sleep is talking to the angels
- bite, don't cut a baby's fingernails for its first year

Of course, the time of birth and configuration of the planets were vital to the baby's personality (*see* **Astrology** *p. 122*). And the day of the birth too was critical (*see over*).

BIRTHDAY RHYME

Monday's child is fair of face,
Tuesday's child is full of grace,
Wednesday's child is full of woe,
Thursday's child has far to go,
Friday's child works hard for a living,
Saturday's child is loving and giving,
But the child who is born on the Sabbath day
Is bonny and blithe, good and gay.

Christening A baby was baptised as soon as possible and to protect it from fairies and evil spirits in its vulnerable, unbaptised state, everything from charms through Bibles to bits of lucky iron were left in its crib. Its first journey in the outside world should be from the house to the church, but once it got there, it was a bad omen if it did not cry during the ceremony, and worse still if it sneezed instead. Parents were often reluctant to let their child be the first one baptised at a new church font, and if there were two babies of opposite sex to be christened, the boy had to go first to avoid his emasculation by the girl; she would, probably for her forwardness and presumption, turn out butch as a result of having been first to the font.

COURTSHIP AND WEDDINGS

The Mating Game The prayer to St Catherine,

patron saint of unmarried women, was a cry of the truly desperate:

St Catherine, St Catherine, lend me thine aid,
And grant that I never may die an old maid.

A husband, St Catherine,
A good one, St Catherine,
But arn-a-one better than
Narn-a-one, St Catherine.

Sweet St Catherine,
A husband, St Catherine,
Handsome, St Catherine,
Rich, St Catherine,
Soon, St Catherine.

Of course, there were ways – other than praying for divine intercession – of finding out who your future spouse would be. Anyone could take a more active part in the question by trying to divine their part-ner-to-be, although these charms would work bet-ter on certain days in the year:

- 20th January (St Agnes' Eve)
- 14th February (St Valentine's Day)

- 21st June (Midsummer Eve)
- 31st October (Hallowe'en)

Ways of divining who your future partner might be included drawing lots with names on; choosing a passage at random from a book for clues; looking for the first person you saw on, for example, St Valentine's Day; and inducing dreams or visions of your intended by performing certain charms with pieces of food, pins or plants, or with a charm in praise of the new Moon:

All hail to the Moon! All hail to thee!
I prithee, good Moon, reveal to me
This night, who my husband [or wife] must be.

Of course, if a woman wanted to cut through the preliminaries and take the situation into her own hands she had only one chance to do it every four years – she could pro-

The model couple: but how many hoops did couples jump through to turn away bad luck?

pose to the man of her own choice every 29th
February, the extra day of the leap year.

The Wedding   There was literally a superstition
for almost every possible decision to be made about a
wedding, and dogmatic ditties dictated to you at every
turn.

... THE DAY

Monday for wealth,
Tuesday for health,
Wednesday is the best day of all,
Thursday for crosses,
Friday for losses,
Saturday no luck at all.

... THE DRESS

Married in white, you have chosen all right
Married in grey, you will go far away
Married in black, you will wish yourself back
Married in red, you wish yourself dead
Married in green, ashamed to be seen
Married in blue, you will always be true
Married in pearl, you will live in a whirl
Married in yellow, ashamed of your fellow
Married in brown, you will live out of town
Married in pink, your fortune will sink.

... THE MONTH

Married in January's hoar and rime,
Widowed you'll be before your prime.

Married in February's sleepy weather,
Life you'll tread in time together.

Married when March winds shrill and roar,
Your home will be on a distant shore.

Married beneath April's changing skies,
A chequered path before you lies.

Married when bees over May blossom flit,
Strangers around your board will sit.

Married in the month of roses, June,
Life will be one long honeymoon.

Married in July with flowers ablaze,
Bittersweet memories on after days.

Married in August's heat and drowse,
Lover and friend in your chosen spouse.

Married in September's golden glow,
Smooth and serene your life will go.

Married when leaves in October thin,
Toil and hardship for you gain.

Married in veils of November mist,
Fortune your wedding ring has kissed.

Married in days of December cheer,
Love's star shines brighter from year to year.

Despite all this advice, it is possible to wed in green on a Saturday in October and still be happily married years later.

Something old, something new,
Something borrowed, something blue.

Before the wedding This particular piece of rhyming advice dictating what the bride should wear has stood the test of changing fashion better than most. Whatever she wore, it should never be seen by her husband-to-be before the service. As the bride left her home for the wedding, she should step over the threshold with her right foot first. It was lucky to see a black cat on the way to the service and to meet a chimneysweep en route was even better (*see p. 32*), but to catch sight of a funeral was the worst of omens.

The ring Few wedding-ceremony symbols are as plain and potent as the wedding ring – made in a circle symbolising eternity and made of gold, the most precious metal. When people could not afford one they borrowed or hired a ring specially for the occasion. It was very bad luck to lose the ring, or drop it during the ceremony, and its owner was discouraged from ever taking it off again once it was on.

After the wedding Confetti-throwing well-wishers would once have thrown rice or nuts, signifying fertility (*see p. 175*). The wedding cake was another sign of luck and fertility and everyone at the celebration had to eat some. An unmarried woman could take some home to sleep with it under her pillow – another way to dream of a future spouse – while the bride also kept some to ensure her husband didn't stray; it was then eaten at their first child's christening celebrations.

DEATH AND BURIAL

Death Omens   Past tradition said that all deaths would be preceded by a sign of some sort, and this was doubtless the case, if only because with such all-encompassing morbidity it was difficult not to be proved right at least some of the time. The list below shows just a few of the enormous range of death omens, usually lurking terrifyingly in the most mundane of incidents.

- a hole in the centre of a loaf
- a dog howling
- furniture creaking
- dropping a comb
- letters crossing in the post
- a diamond-shaped fold in a sheet or tablecloth
- opening an umbrella indoors
- ringing in your ears

Dying   Once death was declared inevitable, doors were unlocked and windows opened to let the soul pass out easily. A dying person lying on a pigeon- or dove-feather mattress or pillow would be moved, at times even onto the floor; some people thought it impossible to die on dove – or pigeon – feather bedding, while direct contact with the floor would make the death-suffering easier.

Death As soon as someone had died, all the knots in the house were untied, mirrors were turned to the wall and any closed doors and windows were flung open. Coins were put on the corpse's eyes to close off any entry route to evil spirits and to ensure the deceased did not see a candidate from among the living to accompany them on their journey (below). Pets were turned out of the house, fires put out and blinds pulled down. All these actions were designed to

ensure an easy passage to Paradise for the deceased's soul:

- so the released soul was not earth-bound, and left to haunt its old home;
- so the soul was not prey to the evil spirits that hovered about the dead;
- so the soul would not take anyone else with it.

After death someone always sat with the body and a light was always kept nearby. These customs gave rise to the practice of the wake, where a cheerful, noisy party would drive away any evil spirits hanging about.

One medieval superstition now almost forgotten is that of the sin-eater: someone, either professional or a dupe, would eat food passed over the corpse. This represented the sins that the dead person had committed during their lifetime, and the sin-eater took on responsibility for them by eating the food.

Funeral   Black was the colour of mourning not just because it was gloomy. As the most unassuming of colours, it would not catch the attention of death, hovering around the corpse and always on the lookout for another victim. This was also a reason to have the corpse buried as soon as possible – it was particularly bad luck to leave a corpse unburied over a Sunday. In any case, many people believed – and many still do – that funerals come in threes.

A funeral procession must never be interrupted or stopped and it is unlucky to join one or attend a funeral without being invited. For their own sake, babies and pregnant women should not attend. The coffin should be carried head first, and must fit into the grave first time, or ill luck would come to all the mourners. Many families still bury loved ones with treasured possessions in the coffin, but in the past it was as likely to have been evil-repelling charms, Bibles, or even coins to pay their passage into the next world.

Rain was a good funeral omen, but a ray of sunlight settling on any one mourner was a dread omen, signifying they were next in line for death.

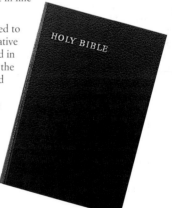

Many families refused to allow their dead relative to be the first buried in a new graveyard, as the Devil always claimed the first corpse in. Likewise, the last to be buried in a

Holy Bible: often buried with the dead to keep them safe from evil spirits

graveyard was obliged to be the ghostly guard of the
cemetery until the Last Call.

OTHER EXPERIENCES AND BEHAVIOUR

While birth, marriage and death were the three
biggies when it came to life and, therefore, superstition, the far more mundane experiences and behav-
iours of everyday life also attracted superstition in
their own right.

Boasting   Possibly the unluckiest thing anyone
could do was to call down the wrath of the gods, or
any of the other ever-vigilant and ever-malicious
supernatural forces, by boasting. Crowing about your
own good fortune was certain to end in a punishment
for presumption, often by removal of the thing you
boasted of. For this reason, boasting about your children was particularly discouraged. The bad luck could
even come passively, through praises and compliments
given by someone else.

Dreaming   One of the commonest forms of future-
telling or wish fulfilment that everyone has access to.
Ancient peoples believed God spoke through dreams,
while the Romans and Greeks thought they revealed
omens, warnings and prophesies – a view still held by
many people today. Another common school of
thought held that dreams worked in opposites: in
other words, what you dreamed of was in direct con-

trast to what would happen. But most people who try to interpret their dreams now see them as a metaphor, either for conflicts in their subconscious or for what might happen in the future. The list below gives some examples of interpretations of common dream types.

THE MEANING OF DREAMS

- **Chasing** if you are chased, you may be running away from a part of your personality you dislike or from a bad situation; if you are chasing, you may be feeling aggressive towards someone
- **Death** surprising news is on the way
- **Driving** you want to exert more control of events
- **Drowning** life is overwhelmingly problematic
- **Embarrassment** strengthen your resolve not to be influenced against your own better judgement
- **Funeral** it is time to move on from a part of life that you want to hold on to
- **Hermit** you need more time to yourself
- **Maze** you are finding it hard to solve a problem
- **Nakedness, Missing clothes** a feeling of inability to face everyday life
- **School** a lack of confidence in your own ability
- **Writing** you need to express your own creativity more

Julius Caesar: his wife had disturbing dreams of the fate awaiting him on the Ides of March

Drowning Not, thankfully, an everyday experience, but one that has some strong associated superstitions. The belief of a drowning person's life flashing by them is still common. It was also believed in the past that the rescuer of someone in danger of drowning would themselves be at great risk of being claimed by the water as its replacement victim. In fact, particular 'killer' rivers around the country, such as the River Dee in Aberdeenshire, were believed to seek out a certain number of drowning victims every year.

Many fishermen in the past never learned to swim,

TOP 10 SUPERSTITIONS: 9

A drowning person sees their life
flash before their eyes

believing the sea would have its victim and that it was pointless to prolong the agonies of drowning.

Although the number three is usually seen as lucky (*see p. 52*), one exception to the rule is in the notion that someone drowning will not go under finally until after they have come up to the surface three times; this is, of course, potentially lethal if would-be rescuers act on it. Any air in the lungs and other natural buoyancy in the body may be expelled as the victim sinks the first time, never to resurface.

Gambling Superstitions about gambling really boil down to a list of dos and don'ts that give you as much luck as possible.

IT'S BAD LUCK TO ...

- drop a card during the game
- become angry
- sing during the game
- lend money to another player
- be touched on the shoulder by a woman during the game or meet a woman on the way to the game (or presumably, be a woman)
- have a hand with the four of clubs in it – the card was called the Devil's Four-Poster
- play with a cross-eyed person at the table
- play on a Sunday or before 6 o'clock in the evening on a Friday

AND GOOD LUCK TO ...

- be a beginner at gaming
- play with borrowed money
- touch a hunchback
- rub your dice on a red-headed person
- stand up and turn around three times with your chair in your hand, to break a run of bad luck (if this does nothing else, it will at least break the concentration of the other players)

Itching Itching or tingling on the body was usually interpreted as a foretelling of something about to happen. Whether this something was good or bad depended totally on what bit of the body was itching. The chart below details what to expect in the wake of any itching body parts.

ITCHY BITS

- **Right hand** you are going to receive money
- **Left hand** you are going to give money away
- **Right eye** good luck is coming to you
- **Left eye** you will suffer some bad luck soon
- **Right ear** someone is saying nice things about you
- **Left ear** someone is spreading lies about you
- **Feet** you will soon be in an unknown place
- **Nose** If your nose itches, your mouth is in danger,
  You'll kiss a fool and meet a stranger

Laughing In the morbidly careworn world of the superstitious, laughing – especially 'to excess' – was always very dangerous, and to be avoided. Prolonged laughter from children would earn a rebuke, as it was a bad omen. In an adult it was even worse, especially if it was out of character, and death was sure to be close to that person. A typical saying warned 'Laughter before breakfast means tears before night'.

Luck   Being lucky or unlucky is the essence of superstition. Most of us have known someone who seems to attract good luck or bad luck to an unusual degree and, especially for the unlucky, their luck never seems to change. Yet ironically, one luck-related superstition is that luck always changes. A lucky break changes a run of bad luck for the better. And beginners at most things, but especially gaming and gambling, also traditionally enjoyed good luck. These are ways of turning aside bad luck:

Crossed fingers can turn aside bad luck

- making a V with your right index and middle fingers, and spitting through them three times
- turning in a circle, clockwise, three times
- making the sign of the Cross
- crossing your fingers

Sneezing   All through history sneezers have benefitted from the blessings of those around them. Sneezing was thought auspicious; some believed life essence was sneezed out with the saliva, others the soul. The circumstances of the sneeze were important.

People standing nearby still greet a sneeze with 'Bless you', 'Gesundheit' or, in Roman days, 'Jupiter preserve you'. In times of plague, sneezing could be a symptom of infection and it was regarded with some dread. More recently, sneezing three times in quick succession was a very good omen, as was two people

---

DAILY SNEEZES

Monday for danger,
Tuesday kiss a stranger,
Wednesday for a letter,
Thursday for something better,
Friday for sorrow,
Saturday, see your lover tomorrow,
Sunday your safety seek,
Or the Devil will have you the rest of the week.

sneezing at the same time. And if you suppress a sneeze, it is a sign that you have a secret admirer. In Scotland, a sneeze from a baby was proof for its parents that their child was not in the power of the fairies. It is lucky to sneeze to the right, especially at the start of a voyage; but trouble lies ahead for someone who sneezes left.

Stumbling   This was always interpreted as much more significant than simply tripping over an uneven road or footpath. The worst-omened stumble and laden with symbolism, was one that happened at the start of any new venture – crossing the threshhold with a new spouse, setting sail on a ship or even your horse stumbling at the start of a journey were all bad omens for the way ahead. Stumbling upstairs foretells a wedding, but stumbling downstairs brings its own bad luck even aside from the physical danger. Worse than this is to stumble at a graveside: the tripper will soon be joining the dead.

Washing   Superstition usually connects dirt with good luck, so washing was a dubious practice at best. It washed away not just the dirt, but the luck, too. Babies' hands were never washed for their first 12 months, and in Scotland clothes were never washed on New Year's Day for fear of washing away the new year's good luck. Good Friday was the unluckiest washing day, as a washerwoman had mocked Christ as he carried the cross to Calvary. Two people washing their hands in the same water were destined soon to quarrel; to counter the bad luck, both had to spit in the water.

Whistling Cheery at best and irritating at worst, whistling was once looked on as a downright foolish thing to do, especially on board ship: whistling imitated the wind, and so could summon it. On the other hand, sailors might whistle gently if they wanted to call up a breeze.

Whistling down a mine and in a theatre were also avoided at all costs – the first would bring an explosion while the second foretold the failure of the play. To whistle in a house would summon up the Devil, and whistling after dark summoned up elemental and evil spirits. But the most infamous whistler of all was a whistling woman.

> *A whistling woman and a crowing hen*
> *Are neither fit for God nor men.*

The official line on this particular prejudice was that a woman had whistled as she watched the nails being forged for Christ's crucifixion. It was also passed on to little girls, who were threatened with unwanted beard growth if they dared whistle.

Yawning The bored or tired sign of the oxygen-starved was long thought perilous: an open mouth was an open invitation to the Devil to enter your body. So originated the custom of covering your mouth with your hand as you yawn. In the past, you might also make the sign of the cross over your mouth, while some Hindus snapped their fingers as they yawned, to shoo away lurking evil. This tradition also extended to certain native Americans, who saw yawning as a sign that death waited nearby to claim you. Again, a snap of the fingers was enough to chase it away.

Types of People

By reason of their status or profession, certain types of people had more than the usual amount of superstitions attached to them.

Actors One of the most superstitious groups of people anywhere. Most of their superstitions are theatre-based and the list opposite shows only a few of the huge number of these.

THEATRICAL BELIEFS

- a perfect rehearsal is a bad omen
- a play's last line must never be said in rehearsal
- a cat in a theatre is lucky, but not if it runs on stage; if it does, however, it is bad luck to kick it
- green and yellow are unlucky colours on stage
- wigs are lucky
- *Macbeth* is unlucky (*see p. 78*)
- *Cinderella* is a lucky panto, *Babes in the Wood* is not
- real flowers must not be used onstage in a play
- having three candles on stage or in a dressing room is unlucky
- it is bad luck to look into the mirror over another actor's shoulder as they put on their make-up
- the same costume should be worn night after night on a successful run of a play

Blacksmiths Their work with elemental fire and magical iron associated blacksmiths with special powers. They were believed to be able to heal sick people and, of course, they married runaway couples at Gretna Green (although other local professions also did the job). Their work with horses made them not just forgers of lucky horseshoes (*see p. 91*), but also keepers of the Horseman's Word, a secret spell that gave total power over horses. (This notion was the basis of the recent book and film, *The Horse Whisperer*.) While several people in a locality might be privy to the secret charm, the blacksmith was usually its 'keeper', officiating over any new inductions into the use of the word.

Children   Most of the best-known superstitions about children specifically concern babies (*see p. 9*). One of the best-known child-related superstitions also relates to the lucky number seven – the belief in the special powers of the seventh child in any family. If this child had a parent who was also a seventh child, and especially was the seventh son of a seventh son, they were believed to have healing powers and the gift of 'seeing', or second sight.

Chimneysweeps   Dirt was seen as lucky, and doubly so when coupled with fire; both these elements made chimneysweeping one of the luckiest of professions – a belief that featured in the Disney film, *Mary Poppins*. Meeting a chimney sweep on the way to your wedding was the best of omens. If you met a sweep at any time you should always greet him, or shake hands.

Sailors   Right up alongside actors in any list of the 10 Most Superstitious, sailors have traditionally attributed superstitious belief to almost every aspect of their work. Perhaps the dangerous nature of the job,

SAILING SUPERSTITIONS

- a ship's name should never be changed and a name ending in 'a' was unlucky
- bad luck will follow if the bottle smashed against the ship's side at its launch fails to break
- children on board are always a good omen
- women and clerics both make unlucky passengers
- a bell ringing by itself on board is a death omen for the ship or its crew
- a ship sails faster while fleeing an enemy
- a shark following a ship is a death omen for someone on board
- a ship carrying a dead body sails more slowly
- seabirds carry the souls of dead sailors
- gold hoop earrings protect the wearer from drowning
- the word 'drown' is never spoken at sea, for fear it summon up the actual event
- whistling, cutting nails and trimming hair at sea are a few of the things that summon up a storm
- horseshoes on a ship's mast turn away storms and shipwrecks; Nelson had one on the *Victory*
- a ship without its figurehead will not sink

where the smallest action done wrongly might lead to disaster, led to the growth of a maze of beliefs, omens and warnings to make sure that absolutely everything was done right. Sailing-associated beliefs have been touched on elsewhere in the book, but the list on page 33 shows just a few of the vast array that exist.

Warriors Most western countries had a superstition relating to the second coming of their national warrior-heroes who would return from sleep, Messiah-like, to rescue their country in its hour of greatest need. For Britain, the greatest hero was Arthur, believed to be sleeping in Avalon, but similar superstitions are attached to others of lesser status. In fact any leader whose death had not been physically witnessed was fair game: Scots and English heroes James IV and Francis Drake, the rebellious 17th-century Duke of Monmouth, heroic General Gordon of Khartoum and Elvis in our own time – a reluctance to believe in the death of our heroes always runs deep.

The Human Body

Almost every part of the body carried its own related superstition.

Blood So essential to the body, blood represented life and the life-force and was even believed to carry the soul – all making it powerful in its own right. It was used to cast charms or spells; it was reputedly used to sign pacts with the Devil; and the blood-sacrifice, as said to have been practised by the Druids, was the most powerful.

The loss of blood was a bad omen. Anyone who bled on Hallowe'en could not expect to live long. Anything from cobwebs through plant roots to urine was applied to a bleeding wound, sometimes with blood-stopping charms to recite:

> As I was going to Jordan Wood
> There was the blood and there it stood,
> So shall thy blood stay in thy body.
> I do bless thee in the name of the Father,
>   the Son and the Holy Ghost.

Nose-bleeds are a special area that still attract superstitious cures today. Most people know that dropping a key (which must be made of iron) down the nose-bleeder's back will stop the bleeding. Less well-known are burning a vinegar-soaked rag then blowing the ashes up the bleeding nose, or wearing a dried toad's body in a bag tied around your neck – although the bleeding would have long stopped by the time these remedies were prepared.

Bone Bones were treated with almost the same reverence as blood and were also used in magic. Healing spells in particular made much use of them, working with bones related to the afflicted area; for example,

Powdered skull – a cure worse than the disease?

- epilepsy sufferers were prescribed powdered human skull, or were advised to drink from a skull bone
- gout was treated with a poultice made up from scrapings of shinbone and earth
- hammering a nail into a skull relieved headaches
- carrying a knuckle-bone about with you protected you from cramp

Eyes & Eyebrows The face's most expressive and revealing feature, the eyes are also the source of one of the most common and long-lasting superstitions – the notion of the Evil Eye, a destructive glance that conveyed bad luck, illness and general harm. It might be

---

THE EYES (AND EYEBROWS) HAVE IT

Beware of those whose eyebrows meet
For in those eyes there is deceit

The eyes are the window of the soul

If your eyebrows meet across your nose
You will not live to wear wedding clothes

SIGNS OF THE EVIL EYE

- eyes of different colour
- deep-set eyes
- eyes set close together
- cross-eyes
- one eye set lower than the other
- left-handedness

done on purpose by witches or other ill-wishers, but it could also be involuntary, belonging even to the most reluctant possessor in spite of their wishes: popes Pius IX and Leo XIII were both said to have it.

Any number of amulets and counter-charms warded off the Evil Eye, the commonest being to spit over your left shoulder or to make the sign of the Cross.

More run-of-the-mill superstitions related to itching eyes (right for good luck, left for bad), twitching eyes (a sign of betrayal) and cures for various eye disorders.

Feet Far more significant than you might think, although in most cases you will have to get someone's shoes off to find out what fate has in store.

- babies born with an extra toe (or two) will be lucky
- babies born feet-first have powers of healing muscle or joint pains in later life, by walking on sufferers

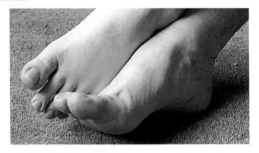

Feet: more to them than just carrying you about

- webbed toes are lucky, except in parts of Scotland where they show the child is a selkie (*see p. 144*)
- flat-footed people are unlucky, especially if you meet them on a Monday or they are a New Year's first foot
- all new beginnings, such as dressing, journeys and newly married life, should begin with the right foot
- itchy feet mean you will soon set out on a journey

Fingers Crossing your index and middle fingers for luck is one of the best-known superstitions, but they can also be crossed to avert evil as you tell a white lie; the MP Tony Banks famously crossed his fingers as he took the Oath of Allegiance in Parliament in 1997.

TOP 10 SUPERSTITIONS: 6

Cross your fingers for luck, especially as you tell a white lie

Pointing is not well regarded in some cultures, where it is a way to bring on the Evil Eye. The first finger is actually called 'the finger of the Evil Eye', or the 'poison finger' in some places, and was not used to apply ointments or healing of any kind. On the other hand, the third finger had healing powers in its touch, simply by stroking; it was believed a vein from this finger ran directly to the heart, which was also why wedding rings were worn on that finger.

Finger shape was also important: long, thin fingers were either a sign of intelligence or of a spendthrift, while short fingers indicated the opposites. A long thumb showed stubbornness but a wide one indicated future wealth. Pricking your thumb is an omen of evil, while an itchy thumb indicates the arrival of visitors. Thumbs up has long been a sign of approval, possibly dating from long before the Roman gladiatorial contests that made it so well known.

Hair Perhaps because it grows from the head and is seen to represent its owner's vigour and vitality, hair was thought to have magical properties. The most famous 'hair story' is the Biblical one of Samson and Delilah, who cut off his hair to rob him of his great strength. Various rules dictated the time of haircuts – not when the moon waned, not in March, not after dark, not when your brother was at sea, not on a Friday, Sunday or Monday. Cuttings were disposed of carefully, preferably by burning, in case they were used for witchcraft or nest-building by a bird of the Dark, such as a magpie.

Curly hair was lucky, and if your hair was straight you could curl it by eating crusts or pouring rum on your head. Curly hair was the sign of an open, cheerful nature, but straight, flat hair denoted a sneaky and deceitful temperament.

Despite many people's long sessions with the blow-dryer and the straightening irons, curly hair really is lucky

Colour, too, was all-important. The old bigotry against redheads is slightly odd but has a long pedigree. Some of history's worst villains have been said to be red-haired, including Judas Iscariot and Rasputin.

A hairy chest meant strength and virility but someone with a hairless chest might become a thief. Hairy arms and hands signalled wealth to come but a hairy back showed stupidity. Someone with a widow's peak could expect long life, and a cow's lick was lucky. Beards, now seen as old-fashioned or slightly eccentric, spoke a whole language of their own. They symbolised virility and authority, but they had to match your hair:

Trust no man, be he friend or brother,
Whose hair is one colour and beard another.

HAIR COLOUR CHARACTERISTICS

- **Blond** fickle and insincere; boastful; resistant to disease; unlucky New Year first foot
- **Red** bad tempered; jealous; passionate; thought possessors of the Evil Eye, or witches
- **Brown** dependable; dull; sincere; healthy
- **Black** hard-working; deceitful; showy; lucky New Year first foot
- **Grey** (early grey) fickle and boastful; but pulling out one grey hair means 10 others grow in its place

Hands Left-handed people were looked on with suspicion, even being thought in league with the Devil; our word 'sinister' comes from the Roman word for 'left'. By contrast, the right hand has always been associated with good: Christ sits at the right hand of God, handshakes are made with the right hand, and even marriages were once made just by clasping right hands. Healing by touch was also done right-handed; for centuries, English monarchs practised a form of faith healing of the disease scrofula, also known as the King's Evil, which involved touching the diseased person with their hand to cure them. The infant Samuel Johnson was treated in this way by Queen Anne. Hand features were important: temperature might be a personality indicator. Most people know 'Cold hands mean warm heart' but it was also said damp hands showed an amorous nature (although this may just have been counter-propaganda by the sweaty-handed).

PALMISTRY

Palmistry studies the hand's features and markings to find out its owner's personality or fate. All parts of the hand are used: shape of hand and palm, mounds on the hand, its proportions and lines, the fingers' relative size, shape, set, span and flexibility, nail shapes, and so on. The left hand indicates a person's potential at birth, while their right hand shows the point they have reached in their life, and what lies ahead. (In a left-handed person, these would be reversed.)

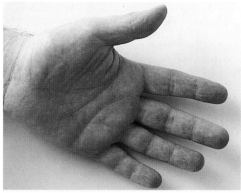

All the features of hand, nails and fingers are studied in a reading, giving an overall picture of a subject's personality

A basic interpretation of hand-shapes in determining a subject's personality might be as follows:

- long, slender hands with long fingers denote an artistic temperament, not given to manual work
- short, stubby hands with short fingers signify a down-to-earth nature and an everyday practicality
- long hands coupled with short fingers belong to a person who is changeable, restless and energetic
- square hands and long fingered-people are clever, rational and like orderliness

Palmistry has been practised for thousands of years – as far back as ancient Egyptian times, and possibly even before that – though it was not always highly regarded and was forbidden by the Church in the 15th century.

Moles   Many people have heard of the Language of Flowers, but the less appealing Language of Moles doesn't enjoy quite such a wide audience. It was believed in the past that moles and birthmarks actually carried a message for human beings, with their position on the body being the key (*see* **Mole Meanings** *opposite*). The illustration

opposite for 17th-century mole-interpreters, with its numbered-grid key to the meanings of facial moles by location, shows just how seriously this belief was taken.

Their interpretation varied; some thought all moles unlucky, while others believed they were the mark of God. Generally, moles on the right side of the body

MOLE MEANINGS

- **Above the eye** early love; many children
- **Right forehead** success; riches; happiness
- **Left forehead** cleverness; sometimes cruelty
- **Cheek** lack of riches; happiness
- **Nose** a far-wandered traveller
- **Mouth** a great eater or talker
- **Ear** contentment
- **Chin** wealth; riches
- **Neck** a hangman's noose beckoned
- **Shoulders** strength of character
- **Arms and hands** difficulties in middle age, followed by comfort and security in later life
- **Stomach** gluttony; strength
- **Legs** poverty; many children

were good-luck omens, while those on the left were bad news. And large, sprouting, hairy moles were said by some to be the luckiest of the lot.

Nails Like cutting hair, cutting nails was not usually a good idea: passing ill-wishers, witches or evil spirits could always use the clippings for their own ends.

It was important not to cut your nails in finger order – that was how a corpse's nails were cut, and to mimic it invited disaster. Large and rounded half-moons at the base were a good sign but if the nails were crooked or clawed their owner was wicked or grasping.

Spots on the nails were significant and, for a change, they usually foretold good luck:

- Thumb: a gift was coming to you
- First finger: friends would come to see you
- Middle finger: an enemy was on the way

Cut nails on Monday you'll get good news,
Cut nails on Tuesday will bring new shoes,
Cut nails on Wednesday and you'll travel,
Cut nails on Thursday and you'll get more shoes,
Cut nails on Friday and there's sorrow,
Cut nails on Saturday and you'll see your lover
   tomorrow,
But cut them on a Sunday and the Devil will get you.

- Ring finger: a letter was on its way to you
- Little finger: you would soon go on a journey

Counting the spots on your nails not only passed the time on a slow evening, in some places it could also tell you how many years you had left to live; in others, it indicated the number of lies you had told.

Shadow Not, strictly speaking, part of the body, but it was treated almost as such. Someone's shadow was in a mysterious way mystically connected with them, almost like their spirit made visible. In ancient Irish legend, the hero Fionn killed his enemy by spearing his shadow. A person's shadow should never be stamped on, and nothing should fall on it. In some places, mourners at a funeral would not stand close to a coffin as the lid was closed in case their shadow might fall inside and be shut in with the body. One particular type of shadow-divination for Christmas Day rather missed the festive spirit: if any of the fire-light shadows was cast without a head its owner would not live to the next Christmas.

Spittle Like blood, spittle had a life-force power and could be used to counter evil charms or to increase the goodness in an action. It also had inherent healing powers: Christ cured a blind man with a paste of spittle and earth. The list on the next page shows that spitting wasn't always thought a disgusting habit.

SPITTING SUPERSTITIONS

- spit on the ground three times to protect yourself from the Evil Eye
- spit on a child to protect them from harm
- spit on your shoe before you start on a journey
- spit on your hands before beginning a fight or hard manual work to make your task easier
- spit when you make a promise or swear an oath to prove you mean what you say
- spit on an insect bite to soothe the inflammation
- to spit over your left shoulder is to spit in the face of the Devil
- spit in a field before you start to gather the harvest, or in a boat before you set sail

Teeth Most famous of the tooth superstitions nowadays is that the tooth fairy visits to leave money in return for a child's newly fallen-out tooth. But she was not always a welcome visitor: in the past, all a person's teeth might be kept to put in their coffin when they died, so they would not go toothless into Eternity. Another option was to burn them to make sure they didn't fall into the hands of a witch.

If a baby was born with a tooth already in place, it signalled a whole range of unpleasant outcomes from bad-temperedness to criminal behaviour. Early teething in a baby indicated there would be another birth in the family soon. A gap between the front teeth meant that the person would be lucky all their lives, but in some areas it was also taken as the sign of an overly amorous nature.

Urine Like blood and spittle, urine had almost magical healing properties and was an enchantment-breaker. As protection against the Evil Eye it was not quite so desirable as spittle; you had to wash your hands in it. This doubled as a cure for chapped hands and, if you paddled in it, chilblains. Rubbing a baby's gums with urine would make sure that it never suffered from toothache in later life (or, if it did, it never let on, presumably in fear of a repeat treatment). Sailors never urinated into the wind, reputedly for fear of the Devil sending a storm, but more likely to avoid getting wet feet.

Warts Frogs and toads were thought to cause warts which may be why traditional pictures of witches, who kept these animals as familiars, always featured a wart or two somewhere. Dipping your hand in water that had been used to hard-boil eggs also gave you warts. There were many suggested cures, but one of the commonest was to steal a piece of meat, rub the warts with it, then bury it. As it decayed in the ground, so would your warts disappear. Others included wrapping red thread around the wart three times, rubbing them with a dead mole (mammal) and dipping your hands in the holy-water font while saying a Hail Mary; in this warty version of Pass the Parcel, your wart would then be passed on to the next dipper.

NUMBERS & WORDS, DAYS & DATES

Names, numbers and related branches of study such as dates and calendars, have always had a special significance in superstition – not least for their importance in charms, spells and the use of magic.

Numbers

From ancient times, all numbers were credited with special power and significance, with odd numbers thought to be the most important. Shakespeare stated, 'There is divinity in odd numbers', and they do have significant attributes and qualities, although, as in the case of 13, these are not always good.

FROM ONE TO NINE

The Greek mathematician and philosopher Pythagoras thought numbers the key to the universe and that the primary numbers – those from one to nine – were the most important of all. The chart on page 52 gives a quick-reference guide to them, with the particularly significant ones receiving more detailed treatment.

NUMBERS & THEIR QUALITIES

1 God, the sun, strength, individuality

2 Duality, balance, harmony

3 One of the most important and multi-faceted numbers; see below

4 Elements, seasons, compass points, squares, foundations, steadiness, practicality

5 The senses, impulsiveness, sensuality

6 Harmony, reliability, tenacity. A perfect number, it is the sum of its factors (1+2+3)

7 The most magical and lucky number; see p. 53

8 Strength of will, reserve, material success

9 Fertility, healing. The sum of three 3s, it will reappear if multiplied (7 x 9 = 63, 6 + 3 = 9). Important in healing and protective charms

Three A number with special magical powers, it was also central in religion. As signified by a triangle, it represented perfect equilibrium, and it was important from Pagan to Christian times, when it came to represent the Holy Trinity. It was associated with luck, but this was not always so. It was important in magic, too: some spells had to have actions or words repeated three times before they would work.

Threes are important in everyday life: people give three cheers, get three chances to get things right, and are granted three wishes. Good and bad luck is often said to come in threes, with a range of events from funerals through weddings, visitors and breakages all falling into this category (*see p. 94* for a typical 'three' superstition).

Seven From the time of the ancients, this has been regarded as a fundamental number. Life was divided into seven ages; astrologers believed seven planets held sway over the universe; a rainbow has seven colours; there were seven deadly sins; a seventh child (especially one born of another seventh child) is often thought to have special powers, including clairvoyance and prophecy. There are seven days in a week; the moon changes from one phase to another every seven days, and the human body and mind is commonly thought to go through quite radical changes every seven years.

SEVENS IN CHRISTIANITY

The world was made in seven days.
There are seven days to the week.
There are seven graces.
There are seven stanzas in the Lord's Prayer.
There are seven ages of man.
Christ uttered seven last words.

These ideas were not just irreligious superstition: the idea of being in Seventh Heaven was an early Islamic concept (being the highest gradation of heaven) and the number was also important to Christians (*see p. 53*).

Although seven is a lucky number to gamblers, it can also accompany bad luck, as with a broken mirror (*see p. 104*). Seven is still the favourite lucky number of most people in Britain.

Thirteen A significant number even before Judas Iscariot gave it such infamy at the Last Supper. It was well regarded by the ancient Egyptians, who believed there were 12 steps on a ladder to eternal life and knowledge; to take the thirteenth meant going through death and stepping over to everlasting life. But by Roman times it had become an ill-omened number of destruction and death. The number was wilfully adopted by witches for their covens, which always number 13, although this may have been a deliberate parodying of the Last Supper. The reluctance to have 13 at table persists – the superstition goes that one

13 *unlucky for some*

TOP 10 SUPERSTITIONS: 1

13 is unlucky and
Friday the 13th is the unluckiest day

diner will die within the year – but its origins are not just Christian. Norse mythology relates the story of a gods' feast to which 12 came, only for Loki, god of mischief and disorder, to gatecrash the event. True to the myth, one of the gods died during the dinner.

Even today, 13 is still avoided at all costs by many people. Most major hotel chains have no room no. 13, and many high-rise buildings have no thirteenth floor (although floor 13 does take centre stage in plenty of ghost and supernatural tales). One of the most famous 13s of modern times was the ill-fated Apollo 13 space mission – on 13 April 1970 its oxygen tank exploded, almost claiming the lives of its three astronauts.

The thirteenth day of the month is an ill-omened day to start any new venture, whether it is a journey, a new job or a wedding. (The exception to the rule is a child born on the thirteenth of the month, who will throughout life enjoy good luck in any new venture begun on the thirteenth.) In particular, Friday 13th is dreaded so much that many people don't even cross the threshold on that day: research has shown there are fewer cars on the road then than on any other

Friday of the year, yet there are more serious car crashes. But in spite of all this, it was revealed recently that thirteen was one of the three most popular numbers chosen in British personalised car number plates.

Other Significant Numbers   In the ancient Greek system, 888 represented the divine, or Higher Mind; this was the number for Iesous, the Greek name of Jesus. The Mortal Mind was represented by 666; in the New Testament, this was the number of The Beast.

NUMEROLOGY

A quasi-arithmetical means to divine the future by the use of numbers, this system dates back over 5000 years with expressions in ancient Greek and some Hebrew mystical systems. It is still studied, although modern practitioners are more concerned with human potential and character analysis than future-telling. Related to astrology, it uses the primary numbers from one to nine as a basis for determining influences on our lives. By finding your birth number from your date of birth, and your name number from the numbers attributed to your name letters, you can gain insights into your own personality and ways to achieve your full potential.

Odd numbers are regarded as masculine, active and creative, while the even numbers are seen as feminine and passive. Ten was seen as the perfect number, as it led back to 1, the source of creation. And the numbers

11, 22 and 33 were never counted down to primary numbers, as they were the numbers of individuals who were spiritually very highly developed.

Birth Numbers To find your birth number, your most important number, add together all the numbers of your birth date. So if you were born on 23 September 1992 you would add 2 + 3 + 9 + 1 + 9 + 9 + 2 = 35; 3 + 5 = 8; this is your birth number which reflects the numerical influences over your birth. The meanings attributed to the number eight show your inherent qualities. (See the chart on p. 52 for an explanation of primary numbers' meanings.)

NAME–NUMBER CHART

1	2	3	4	5	6	7	8	9
A	B	C	D	E	F	G	H	I
J	K	L	M	N	O	P	Q	R
S	T	U	V	W	X	Y	Z	

Name Numbers Representing your acquired, changeable traits, the name number is less important than the birth number. If the name number and birth number are the same, it reflects a harmonious personality. In calculations, use the name you are normally known by.

Days & Dates

If numbers ruled the universe and the affairs of humanity, it was logical that days and dates were viewed as having their own particular characteristics.

WEEKDAYS

Good days and bad days dictated the success or failure of almost any undertaking, and it was important to know what days of the week would bring the best luck for what you wanted to do. In times past there was hardly a day of the year that someone, somewhere didn't regard as unlucky.

The charts on the pages that follow show how some days were lucky or unlucky for certain activities – sometimes even the same ones – but the rhyme below is the best-known of all weekday-related superstitions.

BIRTHDAY RHYME

Monday's child is fair of face,
Tuesday's child is full of grace,
Wednesday's child is full of woe,
Thursday's child has far to go,
Friday's child works hard for a living,
Saturday's child is loving and giving,
But the child who is born on the Sabbath day
Is bonny and blithe, good and gay.

MONDAY

past events & omens	Three of the unluckiest days of the year were Mondays: • Sodom and Gomorrah were destroyed (2nd Mon in August) • Cain murdered Abel (1st in April) • Judas was born (last in Dec)
general beliefs	'As Monday does, so goes all the week' – Monday's events, good or bad, dictated the week's pattern
do	Little could be recommended here – Monday's unlucky associations meant few things begun then were certain to be successful
don't	• move house on this day • begin any new enterprise • make any pledges or promises • get married • ask favours from friends • wear emeralds
lucky gemstone	Pearl
ruling planet	The Moon

TUESDAY

past events & omens
There were no specially bad omens for this day, but its relationship to Mars meant that Tuesday was generally regarded as unlucky

general beliefs
Its combative associations meant Tuesday was seen as a day likely to bring quarrels and disputes

do
- begin any war, legal dispute or other combat on this day (but see don'ts)
- start or sign up to business deals
- get married (but see don'ts)

don't
- start any war or combat (a Middle Eastern belief)
- move house on this day
- begin any new enterprise
- make any pledges or promises
- get married (but see dos)
- ask favours from friends
- wear emeralds

lucky gemstone
Ruby

ruling planet
Mars (the Red Planet, and also the god of War)

WEDNESDAY

past events & omens
Muslims believe God created light on the third day, so this is a lucky day for them

general beliefs
Wednesday is generally thought lucky –
- in spite of the Birthday Rhyme (*see p. 58*), some consider this the best day to be born
- if the sun doesn't shine on this day, a bad storm is omened
- a new moon is very unlucky

do
- communicate by any means: letter, phone, fax or e-mail
- make short trips
- begin medical treatments

don't
- get married
- commit yourself to costly purchases
- wear new gloves

lucky gemstone
Sapphire

ruling planet
Mercury

THURSDAY

past events & omens
In the Middle East, this is thought a lucky day, although not in the west

general beliefs
Thursday is seen as an unlucky day, with only the hour before the dawn bringing any good. Despite this, it is an auspicious day to undertake any hard or responsible tasks

do
- get married
- accept new responsibilities
- make important decisions
- undertake difficult tasks

don't
- begin a new job
- start at a new school
- eat chicken
- spin wool
- undertake any manual labour
- wear emeralds

lucky gemstone
Garnet

ruling planet
Jupiter

FRIDAY

past events & omens

Traditionally seen as the unluckiest day of the week, with some catastrophic past events –

- Adam and Eve ate the apple and were cast out of Eden
- The Great Flood began
- The Temple of Solomon fell
- Christ was crucified

general beliefs

There are so many Friday-related beliefs that it merits a separate section (see p. 66)

do

Few undertakings are well begun on a Friday, and even those that are have contradictory advice –

- cut your nails or hair
- wear new clothes

don't

- get married
- start a new job
- start out on a long journey
- open a new play

lucky gemstone

Emerald

ruling planet

Venus

SATURDAY

past events & omens	The day of Shabbat, and the day God created man
general beliefs	The sun will always shine at some time on a Saturday, although many people still consider it an unlucky day. A new moon on a Saturday is especially unlucky
do	• tell Friday night's dreams, to have them come true • make journeys
don't	• move house – 'Saturday flitting is a short sitting' • leave hospital; Irish hospitals try not to discharge on this day • do voluntary or charity work • work long hours • get married • undertake any new venture
lucky gemstone	Diamond
ruling planet	Saturn

SUNDAY

past events & omens	The day of the Resurrection, considered the greatest of days by Christians
general beliefs	For its association with the Resurrection, Sunday is the luckiest day for anything
do	• take on new responsibilities on this day • get married • attend church • sing • rest from work
don't	• do any labour, other than voluntary work • turn a bed or change the sheets • begin medical treatments • cut your nails or hair
lucky gemstone	Yellow gemstones
ruling planet	The Sun

Friday Friday was traditionally regarded as a day when any bad event would take place.

> *Now Friday came. Your old wives say*
> *Of all the week's, the unluckiest day.*

Criminals traditionally would be reluctant to choose a Friday as the day to commit their crime, as it was sure to fail and they would be arrested. Friday sentencing was thought to be harsher than on any other day of the week, and it was also known as Hangman's Day because executions were usually held then. In fact, anyone taking a case to court that day would be likely to lose.

It is a bad day to start a courtship; singing on a Friday will bring tears on a Sunday; and rain on a Friday foretells good weather the following Sunday. A baby born on a Friday might have a Bible laid in its crib to ward off evil, although in some places Friday was thought a good day to be born. The Church calendar, with its encouragement of Friday abstinence, added to the general Friday-inspired gloom. And of course, Friday 13th is the most unlucky day (*see p. 55*).

Ships rarely set out on a Friday, although this was contradicted by Christopher Columbus – he not only set sail on a Friday, he also saw the New World for the first time on that day.

MONTHS

Months are also associated with many superstitions, some of which are listed below.

January	• 'A warm January means cold to May'
	• 'A mild January means bad luck for man and beast'
	• January was named after Roman god Janus: being two-headed, he could see both behind and ahead
February	• Italians considered February an unlucky month
March	• A wet March means a bad harvest
	• A cold, dry March will be good for crops
	• A March wedding will bring joy and sorrow
April	• April Fool's Day is celebrated with practical jokes every April 1st
	• No tricks can be played after 12 noon; then the victim can retort:

April Fool's gone past,
You're the biggest fool at last.

May	• May is the Virgin Mary's month
	• May Day has been an important holiday since time out of mind (*see p. 72*)
	• Washing your face in the May dew ensures good skin for the coming year
	• May blossom brought into the house is unlucky
	• It is an ill omen to marry in May
June	• The luckiest month for weddings, a belief possibly from the 1st June feast of Juno, Roman goddess of women, marriage and birth
July	• July was believed to be the year's unhealthiest month (*see p. 121*)
August	• 'If the 24th of August be fair and clear, Then hope for a prosperous autumn that year'
September	• The seventh month of the Roman year, it was regarded as lucky
October	• Hallowe'en is celebrated every 31st October (*see p. 73*)
	• Many omens of death and futuretelling surround Hallowe'en

November	• An ill-omened month, November marked the onset of winter proper
December	• Traditionally the time of midwinter celebrations to ward off the dark, including the Norse festival of Yule and the Christian Nativity

DATES

It was not just days and months that had superstitions attached; at a time when omens and reasons were looked for in the tiniest of events, particular dates took on huge significance. These dates were often personal to families or even individuals, and many people kept a record of what days were lucky or unlucky for them. One of the best known of these is 3rd September, which Oliver Cromwell regarded as his lucky date. On it, he won two of his great military victories, yet oddly it also proved to be his death date. In fact, it has been important throughout British history, witnessing among other things the Great Fire of London in 1666 and the outbreak of the Second World War in 1939.

Other dates were also generally agreed to be good or bad (for example, *see* **Monday** *p. 59*) and there were usually a few auspicious dates every month. Those that were considered to be unlucky were often called Egyptian days, supposedly after the plagues that struck Egypt during the time of the Israelites' captivity.

NOTABLE DATES

	☺	☷
January	4 19 27 31	1 2 5 10 13 15 17 23 29
February	7 8 18	2 8 10 17 21
March	3 9 12 14 17	1 13 15 16 20 23 28
April	5 18 27	10 16 20 21 29 30
May	1 2 4 6 9 14	7 10 15 17 20
June	3 5 7 9 12 23	1 4 8 20
July	2 6 10 23 30	5 13 15 21 27
August	5 7 10 14 19	2 13 20 27 31
September	6 10 15 18 23 30	7 13 16 22 24
October	13 16 20 31	3 6 9 15 27
November	3 13 17 23 30	6 15 20 25
December	10 20 29	6 9 15 28 31

☺ = *lucky*   ☷ = *unlucky*

FEASTS AND FESTIVALS

The festivals listed here are the ones that most significance and superstition were attached to.

New Year's Day Celebrated in anticipation of the promise of the year ahead, the optimism of New Year celebrations is summed up in the tradition of making New Year's resolutions. And there were lots of superstitions relating to the death of the old year and the birth of the new.

Opening the windows just before midnight let out the old bad luck and caught the new year's good fortune. Any fire in the grate must be kept burning, and everyone made sure their pockets were not empty, or a year of want would lie ahead. Midnight was celebrated with ringing bells and noise to drive away evil spirits.

The first person into the house on New Year's Day, the first-foot, had to be a dark man, preferably tall and handsome, bringing a piece of coal and some cake. Unfortunately for this gift-bearing hunk, anyone giving a present on this day was also thought to give away their luck, although to lend something was very lucky. Nothing was taken out of the house on this day in case good luck went out, too. Cleaning your chimney brought good luck through the year, although washing clothes was to be avoided at all costs. A favourite New Year pastime to divine the future was to close your eyes and pick out Bible verses using a pin.

Easter The greatest day of the year for Christians, Christ's resurrection is traditionally celebrated on the first Sunday after the full moon after 21st March. The name comes from Eastre, Saxon goddess of spring and the dawn; her sacred animal was the hare – itself deeply involved in Easter custom and celebration.

EASTER SUNDAY CUSTOMS & BELIEFS

- the sun dances in the dawn sky
- anyone looking through dark glass at the sun will see the Lamb and Flag in its centre (see p. 141)
- lamb is the traditional dish in honour of Christ, the Lamb of God
- wearing new clothes or a new hat in honour of new beginnings brings good luck
- painted, hard-boiled Easter Eggs are rolled down a hillside: the eggs are a symbol of life, the painting symbolises Christ's blood, and the rolling recalls the stone rolling away from Christ's tomb
- Eastre's sacred animal was the hare, which was supposed to bring eggs for children; the modern-day egg hunts derive from this, as does the US tradition of the Easter Bunny
- the Easter lily represents purity and is a symbol of the Virgin Mary and newly resurrected Christ
- holy water gathered today has great efficacy

April Fool's Day According to some authorities, the fooling and tricking of April Fool's Day are not as old as some other customs and may have started in the 17th century. Victims were sent on a fool's errand, had practical jokes played on them or were tricked into believing a ridiculous story. The last of these is the type that mainly survives to the present day.

Mayday This festival took over from the traditional Celtic fire-festival of Beltane, celebrated for the returning summer. The tradition of dancing round the beribboned May Pole (usually a hawthorn tree stripped of its branches) was an ancient one that was taken very seriously – one maypole in London was recorded as being over 130 feet high. Under Cromwell's rule such godless celebrations were banned. Traditional celebrations always saw the crowning of a Queen of the May, and all the rites of Mayday were intended to bring fertility, a good grow-ing season for the crops, and good luck.

Nowadays the Mayday holiday has changed emphasis, to become a Europe-wide holiday for all workers.

Hallowe'en Its full name is All Hallows' Eve – the eve of All Saints' Day, on 1st November. It was also the last day of the year in pagan times, the day of the dead. It was thought that the spirits of the dead, evil spirits and demons roamed the earth; more lately it was believed that all souls in Purgatory were set free for 48 hours. If you were out walking at Hallowe'en

and heard footsteps behind you, you must not turn round for death was stalking you. Hunting was not advised on Hallowe'en for fear of wounding a passing soul. The associations with the dead and with evil spirits live on today in the jack-o'-lantern carved pumpkins and turnips, as well as the witch and demon dress-up costumes.

There were hundreds of ways to predict the future on Hallowe'en; some are listed here.

HALLOWE'EN PREDICTIONS

- nuts, symbols of life and fertility, were named after would-be lovers and thrown on the fire. If one jumped, that lover would be unfaithful but if it burned it showed the named one's love was true, and if two burned together, the named pair would be married

HALLOWE'EN PREDICTIONS

- to find your spouse's initial, peel an apple in one long strip and throw it over your shoulder; the peel will fall in the shape of the initial

- if a young woman ate an apple as she combed her hair in front of a mirror, she would see the image of her future husband behind her shoulder

- to find the status of the person you would marry, you would be blindfolded and led to three cups on a table. To choose the one with fresh water indicated a young, unmarried spouse; the dirty water meant your partner would be a widower or widow; and the empty one meant a single life beckoned

Christmas The latest and most-celebrated in a long line of mid-winter festivals that date back to pagan times. Innumerable superstitions surround Christmas, some of the most enduring from pre-Christian times.

Greenery was brought into the house for good luck and good cheer and to show the continuation of life in the depths of winter. Nowadays it is common to take down any Christmas decoration, including the tree, just after New Year, whereas previously it was bad luck to take them down not just before the 12 days of Christmas were up, but before Candlemas Day, on 2nd February.

The holly and the ivy: traditional greenery for Christmas

The tradition of burning the Yule Log was a Europe-wide one that had its roots in the great pagan fire-festivals of midsummer and midwinter. Another reminder of life's continuity in the depths of winter, the log was not allowed to burn down during Christmas' 12 days. It kept evil from the door and welcomed with light and heat dead family members, who were believed to revisit their loved ones at Christmas. A piece of each Yule Log was kept as kindling to light the next year's fire.

Like Hallowe'en, Christmas was a magical time with plenty of associated superstitions and future-telling.

CHRISTMAS SUPERSTITIONS

- at midnight, animals kneel and are given the gift of speech to tell one another the good news
- at midnight, doors were opened to let out evil
- at the consecration of midnight Mass, the souls of the dead could be seen in procession outside
- on Christmas morning, the first visitor to the house must be male
- Christmas engagements ensure a happy marriage
- a woman standing under the mistletoe must kiss any man who came by; to refuse meant bad luck
- many-berried holly in the home kept out evil
- all family members stirred the pudding sunwise

Words

THE IMPORTANCE OF NAMES

Basic to any living thing and as much a part of them as their body or soul, was their name. It was the key to power over that person and was even kept secret in some circumstances. Names could be changed to redirect good or bad luck, certain people with special names were thought to have particular powers, and even to say the name of something considered unlucky was to risk bringing some of that ill-luck on yourself.

As names were potentially so powerful, they had to be used with great care. If you spoke about a dead person, you had to be careful not to summon their spirit to you; so any naming of them was followed up with a quick 'God rest his soul' or 'May he rest in peace'. The same precautions were taken with the fairies, who were more usually called the Little Folk or the Good Neighbours. The same euphemisms are still used today but for different dread subjects: cancer is the Big C and death is a passing away or falling asleep. And many actors and theatrical types, including Sir Richard Attenborough, would rather do anything than name *Macbeth*. Called instead The Scottish Play, it is regarded as very unlucky, with accidents, fires and even deaths attributed to its evil influence. This is said to come from the witches' song, which they believe can work powerful dark magic. Some other types of names were also very important.

Children's Names Because witches could cast a spell over someone just by knowing their name, a newborn's name might be kept secret from everyone but the parents and godparents right up to the very moment of its christening. It was very unlucky to give a child the name of a sister or brother who had already died, in case that one should die, too. Seven-letter names were the luckiest, but if your chosen name or name-combination had 13, you would be advised to alter it to give yourself more or less letters.

Godly parents might choose a name at random from the Bible, or call their child after an especially loved or respected saint, hoping to acquire some of that person's qualities as well as their divine care. Nowadays, less godly parents might also call their child after a rock star, film star or an entire football team, while for the less star-struck, there are hundreds of babies' names books detailing every smallest name meaning, to help parents in their all-important choice.

Married Names Where a woman was to change her surname on marriage, it was very ill-omened to use her new name, or even write it down to see what it looked like, before the wedding itself. This was seen as tempting the gods, and the marriage was certain not to happen. On the other hand, if she were called by her old name after her wedding, that was a bad omen for the new marriage. And a woman with the same maiden name and married name, or one who was twice married to two unrelated men with the same surname, was thought to have healing powers: to take a piece of buttered bread from her hand was thought a certain cure for whooping cough and other infectious diseases. Finally, if her married name could not be the same as her maiden one, it must be quite different, as this ominous little rhyming couplet must have reminded many brides-to-be:

Change the name but not the letter,
Is a change for worse instead of better.

Sailors & Names   As some of the world's most superstitious people, sailors naturally have plenty of omens to read into the use of names. Names ending in 'a' were usually considered bad luck – the *Lusitania*, torpedoed in the Atlantic in 1915, is a classic example – although this belief may be out of favour, as some of the world's most luxurious liners have names that end in 'a'. But it would bring worse luck to re-name an already-named ship. And whole groups of people and things were never named on board: everything from parts of the body to women, animals, bits of the boat itself through to priests and ministers.

OTHER WORDS

Naming was not the only powerful way to use words: spells and charms made use of words of power, while curses used them for altogether more sinister ends.

Abracadabra   There is a tired old joke about a mother who tries to get her child to say 'please' when he asks for things. She will not give him his biscuit until he asks properly, and prompts him with 'What's the magic word?' only to have the reply, 'Abracadabra'.

Unfunny as it is, the joke shows not just how long the word has lasted, but how it is still a familiar part of our language. It is associated now mostly with cod magic and stage magicians but it was once thought that simply saying 'abracadabra', like an invocation for divine protection, would summon up great powers. Its earliest-recorded use was in the 2nd century AD, when saying it was recommended as a cure for fever. It was said to be a corruption of old Hebrew words for Father, Son and Holy Spirit, but this is not very likely, and its true origins may well date from before the time of Christ.

It was also a powerful counter-charm against illness and misfortune: believers had to write down the word several times on paper which they then wore in the shape of a cross round their neck. It should be written with two fewer letters each time and set in the form of an inverted triangle:

abracadabra

bracadabr

racadab

acada

cad

a

When it was thrown away at the end of the allotted time, the misfortune would be thrown away with it.

Charms Sometimes objects but often magical chants, said to protect against ill-wishing or bad luck, or to call in good luck or health. The power of the words used in the charm would accomplish whatever it set out to do, as in this charm to cure a burn:

Two angels came from the west,
One brought fire, the other frost.
Out fire, in frost.

Curses   In these millennial, post-*X-Files* days, old-
fashioned curses now go under the altogether more
interesting name of Psychic Attack. The purely verbal
type of ill-wishing or cursing calls down evil powers
against a perceived enemy, and in the past it was taken
very seriously. It had a long pedigree: the Church used
and encouraged it, from the pope right down to
parish clergy, who could also be petitioned to use it by
one parishioner against another. God-fearing people
prayed on bended knee to visit their enemies and their
families and houses with death and destruction. One
of the most powerful examples was the Beggar's Curse
– the calling down of divine vengeance on those who
would not give alms. There was a widespread belief in
the power of this curse right up into the 19th century.

Cursing was a double-edged sword: always invoked by
the powerless against the powerful, it was called the
work of the Devil when it seemed to work.

Shapes

Like words and numbers, shapes were used to symbolise the world; some were also objects of power in
their own right.

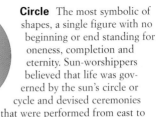

Circle The most symbolic of shapes, a single figure with no beginning or end standing for oneness, completion and eternity. Sun-worshippers believed that life was governed by the sun's circle or cycle and devised ceremonies that were performed from east to west in its honour. Evil spirits were believed not to be able to get into a circle, but the shape was both inclusive and exclusive: just as no spirit or witch could cross a circle, so an outsider could not enter a circle drawn by a witch to perform her magic inside; but if the witch accidentally crossed over the edge, disaster would result.

A circle could be drawn around a new mother's bed, to protect her and her baby from evil; the vulnerable sick might also get the same treatment. It was reproduced in Native American medicine wheels, in stone circles and in mandalas. Circles are still used today, in wedding rings, dance movements and even the shape of the Communion bread.

Triangle Great significance was once attached to the triangle: it had deep religious significance, suggesting the Holy Trinity, and was also a strong shape architecturally. Iron nails might be hammered into a house or barn door in the shape of a triangle to ward off witches or the Evil Eye. Of course, the Egyptians used the triangle in its three-dimensional form for the construction of their pyramids, whose shape they believed awakened the sleeping god in the soul of the dead. In our own time, it has been said the pyramid shape concentrates other energy, so reviving ailing plants and blunt metals, relieving headaches and burn pains, and aiding sleep and meditation.

Colours

Almost all the colours had their own particular association, as some still have today: for example, black is still usually regarded as the colour of mourning, although nowadays it is worn in any number of other situations. The colours listed here had particularly strong associations in superstition.

Green Good and bad luck were both attributed to green. For the most part it was a colour people tended to avoid wearing: the chosen colour of the fairies, it would have been bad luck to upset them by copying it. It was also bad luck to wear it at a christening or onstage (some actors refused even to wear it at all) and for a bride to wear it at her wedding. On the other hand, one Irish custom called for a green tree branch to be fixed to the wall of a house on May Day to ensure good milking throughout the year. And green has been the colour of continued life and of resurrection.

Red The colour of blood and fire, red has had some negative associations in the west. Prejudice against the red-haired and red-bearded is centuries old. But it was also a colour that was thought to drive away the Devil and evil spirits and was often used as protection: so, farmers would tie red ribbons around cows' tails before they let them back out to pasture in the spring; a rowan cross tied with red thread (*see p. 159*) gave excellent protection against the Evil Eye; and a popular superstition until quite recently was to tie a red ribbon somewhere inside a new car, for luck. (Incidentally, red-letter days came from the church's liturgical calendar which featured saints' days, special feast days, in red; all the other days were printed as usual in black.)

White Innocence, purity, simplicity and truth were the qualities represented by white. It has been the colour of religious ceremonial robes since the time of the Druids and is still the colour that most first-time brides choose to wear at their wedding. New babies are also dressed in it, especially for their christening. But it was not totally without negative connotations: white was the chosen colour of mourning the death of Caesar in ancient Rome, and it is still the traditional mourning colour in China today.

Yellow Traditionally the colour associated with cowardice, betrayal and death. It was painted on the doors of French traitors; it was used to describe those who were thought cowardly; it is a colour Judas Iscariot was often depicted wearing; and it was the colour of the Star of David that the Nazis made their Jewish victims wear. Yet yellow was also the colour of gold and of the sun.

OBJECTS

This is the group of superstitions that has proved the most lasting. The habits of farm animals, the importance of weather patterns and the usefulness of plant lore have all lost their former significance but everyday objects still hold a superstitious pull over most of us.

Everyday Objects

AMULETS

An amulet or charm is anything used to ward off evil or bring good luck. From a sportsman's 'lucky jersey' to a motorist's medallion of St Christopher, it is any object its owner credits with the power to protect or bring luck. On the next few pages are some of the commonest ones.

A 'lucky' football top might stay unwashed for weeks

*Any bell ringing by itself
can still evoke dread*

Bells Ringing bells, especially church bells, drove away evil spirits – although a church bell ringing of its own accord is an omen of death for a parishioner. A modern version of this omen says a ringing phone with no caller on the other end foretells bad news. Although the digital tone-telephone, with no bell inside, has dented the power of this superstition, some people still feel dread if their phone – or any other bell – rings for no apparent reason.

Bible As the holiest book in Christendom, the Bible was often used, especially after the Reformation, as a protective amulet. Sleeping with one under your pillow gave protection from the powers of darkness (although not a comfortable night), while in Scotland a Bible in a baby's crib protected it from abduction by fairies.

Bibles were also used to foretell the future. Someone who wanted to know how the new year would go for them would open the Bible at random on 1st January, stick in a pin or point their finger at the open page, then try to interpret whether the chosen verse meant good or bad luck for the next year. Anyone facing a dilemma or problem could use the same method. King Charles I tried it during the Civil War and successfully foretold his own black future.

Birthstones From ancient Egyptian times down to the present, precious and semi-precious stones have been thought to have special powers they can pass on to a wearer. Each of the 12 months also has its own stone that is lucky for someone born in that month.

BIRTHSTONES & THEIR QUALITIES

- **January** Garnet for faithfulness
- **February** Amethyst for sincerity and moderation
- **March** Bloodstone for courage
- **April** Diamond for innocence and purity
- **May** Emerald for happiness and contentment
- **June** Pearl or agate for long life
- **July** Ruby for courage and purity
- **August** Sardonyx for personal happiness
- **September** Sapphire for wisdom
- **October** Opal for hope; this stone is very unlucky for those born in other months
- **November** Topaz for faithfulness
- **December** Turquoise for wealth and success

Four-leafed Clover Clover, with its three-leafed association with the Trinity always brings good luck to its wearer (*see p. 163*). But luckier still is the rare four-leafed type – if it is given away the same day it's found the finder is promised true love. Eve was said to have stolen a four-leafed clover from the Garden of Eden before she was cast out (not so lucky for her). Druids believed it helped them see evil spirits, and for centuries it was used as an evil-repellent that also let the bearer see fairies.

Holy Artefacts Relics and holy medals, especially blessed ones, are said to bring the protection of the featured saint to the person wearing them. Medallions of St Christopher, patron saint of travellers, can still be found adorning many car dashboards, overseeing each journey. Holy water has particular powers against evil, especially if collected in Holy Week although surprisingly, with the exception of water from the shrine at Lourdes, not many curative powers are attributed to it. One of the few is that dipping your hands in it will cure warts – perhaps a reason why much holy water, stagnant so long and used by so many, was recently found to be a hotbed of germs and bacteria.

Horseshoes Despite the demise of the horse, this is still one of the luckiest items known to humanity. Forged by a black-smith (a lucky trade) out of elemental fire and made of iron (*see p. 92*), it was not only a lucky U-shape but was held in place by seven iron nails – seven being the luckiest number (*see p. 53*). They were nailed over barn or house doorways, although it was never settled whether ends up or down was best. Ends up catches good luck, ends down lets the good luck flow out over your door and stops evil entering in.

TOP 10 SUPERSTITIONS: 7

Horseshoes are lucky

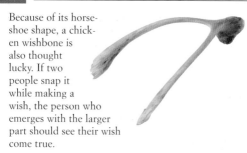

Because of its horse-shoe shape, a chicken wishbone is also thought lucky. If two people snap it while making a wish, the person who emerges with the larger part should see their wish come true.

Iron With its strength to crush bronze and stone and ability to withstand fire, iron has been credited with magical properties from prehistoric times, and its association with good magic continued long beyond then. It terrified evil spirits, witches and fairies and warded off the Evil Eye, so it was used as an amulet in the home. An iron horseshoe (see p. 91) might be nailed over the door, iron nails used to build a crib, and pieces of iron were secreted around the house.

Iron had curative powers, too: iron nailed to a tree after touching the afflicted part of a sick person's body would take the sickness with it. But it should never touch a plant with healing powers, as the plant would lose its own power.

Mascots Most of us have some lucky item or talisman, even one we regard half-jokingly, that we carry around or keep at home. Through history, people, animals, birds and objects have all been used as lucky mascots. The Roman armies carried their luck-bringing eagle on their standards, the Crusaders bore the Cross, and native Americans had their totem poles. Being invested with trust and hope meant that many mascots came to represent the spirit and essence of their owners: this is easily seen nowadays, from the animal mascots of various army regiments, to the image of Britannia in Britain or of the American bald eagle in the US.

Rabbit's Foot   Associated with the return of spring and with fertility, rabbits (*see p. 143*) and hares (*see p. 142*) were long thought lucky animals. As they ran, their back feet touched the ground ahead of the front. This unusual gait made the hind feet especially lucky but in today's more ecologically aware times the tradition of carrying around a severed rabbit's or hare's foot, while not exactly unknown, is far less popular.

Bringing luck, but not to its original owner: a lucky rabbit's foot

OTHER IMPORTANT OBJECTS

These items don't bring good luck in the way that amulets do, but each carries its own significance in the world of superstition, omen and tradition.

Cigarettes   A modern-day superstition is that it is unlucky to light three cigarettes off one match – ill luck will come to the third smoker. Variations on this belief pre-date the 20th century, although it came to prominence in the trenches of the Western Front during the First World War: a match lit long enough to light three cigarettes gave an enemy sniper time to line up his shot. The belief later spread to the civilian population and, to his misfortune, was referred to jokingly by King Alexander of Greece in 1920, when he and

two friends smoked cigars lit from one match. Just days later the king was dead from an infection contracted from a monkey bite.

Money   Symbol of wealth and its trappings – power, strength and attractiveness. Many sayings and superstitions surround it; some of them are listed opposite.

MONEY BELIEFS

- a coin in a new purse or wallet brings good luck
- a coin put in a baby's pram or crib will bring good luck and wealth
- to find a coin means more wealth will come
- putting the first coin you receive each day into an empty purse or pocket will let it attract more
- coins with holes in them are especially lucky
- tossing a coin to solve a dilemma lets the gods or Fate decide the matter for you
- money is the root of all evil *(proverb)*
- money makes the world go round *(proverb)*

Ships Sailors are among the most superstitious of people and virtually every element of sailing and ships has some superstitious ritual attached. Female figureheads and eyes that traditionally adorned ships were there to frighten away evil spirits. If a curse had been put on a ship, it could be lifted by spitting on board. A ship begins its life once it is named, but if this is done with a bottle smashing against its side, it must break at the first blow to avoid bad luck. Any naming must not be done by a pregnant woman or the ship will never return home. In fact, women were bad news generally as far as sailors were concerned: even to have a woman as a passenger was to invite ill luck.

Shoes Strangely, there are many shoe superstitions. You should always put on your right shoe before your left; you must never sneeze as you put on your shoes; and it is a bad sign if you put a shoe on the wrong foot. To forget to tie both laces is lucky, but it is bad luck if only the left lace is untied. Leaving shoes on a chair foretold an argument in the house – although this might have been with someone whose clothes got dirty after sitting in the chair. And if your shoes squeak, this is a sign that they have not been paid for!

Many shoe superstitions are wedding-related. Tying old boots to the newlyweds' car bumper is well known, but this is an updated version of the old custom where the bride's father threw a shoe after the departing pair

– possibly from times when brides were 'stolen' by feuding families. The bride's practice of throwing her bouquet is also recent: she used to throw a shoe, to be caught by the person who would marry next.

Umbrellas

One of the best known of all superstitions is that an umbrella must never be opened indoors for fear of bringing bad luck on its owner and the household. This may come from the umbrella's original purpose as a sunshade; to use one of these indoors would have been taken as a deliberate insult to the sun.

Umbrellas are vaguely unlucky items generally: it is bad luck to give one as a gift; whoever drops one must never pick it up (if a single woman does this, she will never marry) – instead, someone else must do it for them. And if an umbrella is opened outside when it is not needed, rain is sure to follow.

Objects in the Home

Many once-common, or still-common household items have attracted superstition over the years.

Bed   Ritual dictated not just how and when a bed should be made, but even how people should get into and out of it. It was unlucky to get in at one side and out at the other – literally, 'getting out of bed on the wrong side'. The position of the bed was important, too: an east–west alignment, following the sun's path, was best; north–south would bring nightmares. Making the bed had to be done by one person in one go, and the bed-maker had to take care what day they turned the mattress. Different days were avoided in different districts, but most common bad-luck days were Friday and Sunday, the Christian Sabbath.

Besom   A traditional sweeping broom is most people's image of a witch's means of transport. But its associated superstitions are far more run-of-the-mill.

Sweeping had to be done into the house, not outwards, for fear of sweeping away all the family's luck. Any upstairs rooms had to be swept by midday: dust swept or carried downstairs

The traditional, broom-twigged besom

after then omened a corpse would soon leave the house that way. And no sweeping was allowed on New Year's Day or Good Friday for fear of foretelling the death of a family member. In some places the expression 'jumping over the besom' means that someone has married – a reference to the old custom of marrying by jumping over a broomstick set across a doorway. But if a single woman stepped over the handle of a besom, she would be sure to be a mother before she became a wife.

Candles The importance of candles in times past is not hard to understand. The only means of lighting the dark hours, they were used not just to see by and during sacred ceremonies but to ward off the ever-vigilant evil spirits. Candles were lit for supernatural protection in childbirth and in death, when they might be set in a ring round the body so spirits could not enter (see p. 83). Candles blessed at the feast of Candlemas on 2nd February were credited with special magical powers.

If a candle burns with a bright spark in the wick, news or a letter will arrive for the person nearest it. A blue candle flame is a death omen, indicating that spirits are nearby. It is bad luck to let a candle burn down and gutter out, but to snuff one out accidentally foretells a wedding. Three candles burning together was unlucky, an earlier forerunner of the three cigarettes lit off one match superstition (see p. 94).

Clocks With their ticking away of life-spans, most clock superstitions are death-related. The children's song *My Grandfather's Clock*, that stops when the old man dies, reflects a popular belief. A change in the rhythm of ticking or the sudden striking of an unwound clock were sure death omens. A death was marked by stopping all the house clocks which were not wound again until after the burial, a tradition featured in the WH Auden poem *Stop All The Clocks*.

Clothes Intimate association with their wearer made clothes prey to charms and spells. Any old item of clothing could be used for ill-wishing. The witches who tried to kill James VI of Scotland in the 16th century went to some lengths to get hold of some of his clothes. It was also thought that to bury clothing belonging to a living person would cause its owner to waste away.

Wearing a piece of clothing inside out by mistake was thought lucky (consolation, perhaps, for someone left label-out and feeling foolish), while to mend or sew a garment while you wore it was to invite bad luck. In less affluent times in the past, someone wearing new clothes could make a wish, but some days were better

than others to give new things their first airing:
Sunday was good, but Easter Sunday was best of all.

Coal The best-known coal superstition is that of
the first-foot, the first visitor to the house on New
Year's Day, bringing a piece of coal with them for
luck. It used to be thought lucky to find a bit of coal
lying on the ground, and many people would carry
these about with them as good-luck charms.

Doors Heavy in symbolism, doors feature in beliefs
relating to birth and death. At both these times the
house doors and windows were opened to allow free
passage of the soul. But after a christening or funeral,
bad luck would follow if people came back in the
same door they had left by; for householders with only
one door, this could sometimes mean coming back in
by the window. But a visitor to the house must leave
by the same way he came in, or all the household luck
would follow him out the door. The best-known door
superstition, however, is that for a happy marriage a
bride should be carried over the doorstep by her new
husband. At her parents' home the doorstep should
also be washed to clean away her footprints, so making sure she will stay in her new home.

Knives This everyday kitchen item was one of the
most important possessions someone could have: used
for hunting, self-defence and fighting and for cutting
up food, it was an essential for survival. The best-

known knife superstition is that to give one as a gift means the relationship will be severed; giving a coin in return by way of 'purchase' would avert this bad luck.

Sharpening a knife after sunset was a bad sign that either a burglar might enter during the night, or an animal would die and the knife would be needed. Dropping a knife on the floor was good luck, and if it stuck in the ground it indicated a visitor would arrive soon. Because knives were made of iron or steel they gave protection against fairies and bad spirits. Knives and daggers were left in babies' cradles for this reason and a knife stuck in a house door turned evil away.

And for many people, leaving knife and fork crossed after a meal is not just bad table-manners, it is a bad-luck omen that should be corrected immediately.

Ladders   One of the world's most widely observed superstitions is the avoidance of walking under ladders. Its origins are obscure: for some, a leaning ladder represents the gallows, so by walking under it you play out your own execution (see opposite). Others say the ladder's angle to the wall and ground forms a triangle, symbol of the Holy Trinity. To walk through

---

TOP 10 SUPERSTITIONS: 3

It's bad luck to walk under a ladder

a triangle violated it, letting yourself fall into Satan's hands. If you walk under a ladder by accident, there are ways to avert a curse.

TO TURN AWAY BAD LUCK AFTER WALKING UNDER A LADDER

- spit three times through the ladder's rungs
- cross your fingers until you see a dog
- spit on your shoe and walk on without looking back until the spit is dry
- reverse backwards out from under the ladder the way you first came in, making a wish as you go out

Laundry Like most housework superstitions, those
to do with laundry regulate the days when it should
and shouldn't be done. Most washing was best done
early on in the week, to allow time to have it finished
and put away before Sunday, the Christian Sabbath;
washing was never done then and many Christians,
particularly fundamentalists, still avoid laundry work
on Sundays.

New Year's Day was a bad day, too: to wash that day
was to wash away a member of your family, and would
bring on a death in the house. The worst of all,
though, was Good Friday. A washerwoman had
mocked Christ on his way to Calvary and in return he
had cursed her and all those who did such work that
day. An old belief was that any laundry done then
would be marked with blood.

In the days of hand-washing, any woman who got her
own clothes wet while washing would surely be cursed
with a drunken husband. It was important also to be
careful ironing: a diamond shape, a 'coffin' ironed into
a sheet or tablecloth, was a death omen for its user.

Mirrors The cause of sleepless nights among the
superstitious and unease even among sceptics, break-

TOP 10 SUPERSTITIONS: 2
Breaking a mirror brings seven years' bad luck

ing a mirror is never an event shrugged off without a thought for the old curse. And although there are many mirror-related superstitions, few are for the good. Almost all share two basic messages – mirrors bring bad luck, and they help tell the future.

For centuries special powers were credited not just to mirrors, but to anything, including metal and still water, that threw a reflection. Shiny and reflective surfaces could be used to divine the future, or to receive messages from the gods. Queen Elizabeth's court magician, John Dee, used a magic mirror for scrying in this way, and he was credited with discovering Guy Fawkes' Gunpowder Plot against King James in 1605. The powers of mirrors and reflections to captivate and deceive have featured strongly in myth and legend through the centuries, from the ancient Greeks' Narcissus (see p. 107) to Snow White's wicked stepmother.

Because mirrors could reflect the future in this way, to break one was to shatter your own future. The only way to turn aside the bad luck was to bury all the

OTHER MIRROR SUPERSTITIONS

- a mirror that falls and breaks by itself is a death omen for someone in the house

- a mirror in a room where a death has just happened must be covered in case the departed soul gets trapped behind the glass; some say the Devil invented mirrors for this

- someone seeing their reflection in a room where a death has just happened will soon die themselves

- in early societies, to dream of or even catch sight of your reflection was a fatal omen

- it is bad luck to see your own face in a mirror by candlelight

- actors believe bad luck will come if they look into a mirror over the shoulder of another

- babies mustn't look in a mirror for their first 12 months or they will not thrive

- if a woman wants to see her future husband, she must eat an apple while sitting in front of a mirror then brush her hair; an image of her husband-to-be will appear behind her shoulder

- if a couple first catch sight of each other in a mirror, they will have a happy marriage; this is one of the very few good mirror omens

The beautiful Narcissus: his obsession with his own image led to his destruction

broken mirror pieces. An alternative but little better omen was that breaking a mirror foretold the death of a family member. It was also thought that to see your reflection was to see your own soul, which is why the undead and vampires, with no soul, have no reflection.

Pictures & Photos   A well-known old superstition was that if a picture in a house fell, a family member would die soon. This idea probably began with portraits, when images of a person were thought to hold something of their essence. Some of these ideas shifted on to photographs, with some primitive people believing that to take their picture was to steal their soul.

Pins   In times past when people made their own clothes, pins were far more commonly used than they are now. Being sharp and made of metal, they were put to use in both witchcraft and protective charms.

As seen in the popular rhymes, picking up a pin was usually lucky but if the point was towards you, it was better to leave it be. Pins were not given as gifts for fear the sharp point would pierce a friendship. But they were thought good protection against witches, and families often built boxes of pins into their house walls or foundations to protect from evil.

An important pin ritual concerned a bride on her wedding night. As her bridesmaids got her ready for bed, they were careful to remove every last pin from her dress. And pins that had been used in a burial shroud must never be used for anything else: they were left in place for burial.

PIN POEMS

See a pin, pick it up,
And all day you'll have good luck

See a pin, let it lie, All the day you'll have to cry

Pick up a pin, pick up a sorrow

Lend a pin, spoil a friendship

Playing Cards Long regarded with distaste and suspicion, playing cards have never been fully accepted as an innocent way to pass the time. Tarot decks were the first known playing cards. They originated in ancient Egypt and their original symbolism is lost, but they were always used to tell the future. The more familiar modern deck is based on the Tarot. Cards' dependence on fate and luck and their encouragement of gambling led many religious-minded to call them the Devil's Prayerbook. Some Christian sects even banned them – although the sickeningly maudlin *Deck of Cards* is a reminder that, like much that is strongly symbolic, playing cards can be interpreted more than one way.

There are almost as many superstitions and traditions surrounding card-playing as there are games:

- Lucky at cards, unlucky in love
- Beginners are lucky at cards
- Borrowed money cannot lose
- Singing or whistling while playing brings bad luck
- Bad luck can be changed by changing the deck
- Never pick up a hand until all the cards are dealt

SIGNIFICANT CARDS

- the four of Clubs is called the Devil's four-poster bed; no hand that has this card can be good
- the ace of Hearts foretells wealth and happiness
- the nine of Diamonds is unlucky; it was used to send the order for the Glencoe Massacre in 1692 and has since been called the Curse of Scotland
- two pairs of aces and eights are called Dead Man's Hand, and are unlucky; Wild Bill Hickok was holding this hand when he was shot dead

Stairs Never pass on the stairs, is a well-known superstition. If it can't be avoided, the people passing should keep their fingers crossed, and speak to each other: keeping quiet makes the situation worse. Tripping up the stairs is a good sign, portending a wedding, but, not surprisingly, falling down the stairs is very unlucky.

Table One of the main table superstitions has an obvious link with the Last Supper: 13 people must never sit down to dine. Either one must leave, or an extra one be invited, or else death will come to one of the diners. No-one should change places once their seat at table has been assigned. If a single woman sits on the table, or is seated at the corner of a table, she will never marry. And if a diner's chair falls over as they get up from the table, they are revealed to everyone to have been lying throughout the meal.

Objects in the Landscape

Superstitions became attached to prominent features in the landscape just as much as to household or everyday objects. Certain places were fearful and avoided at all costs; others were seen as places of sanctuary and safety in a threateningly unpredictable countryside where hidden dangers might lurk behind any rock.

Bridges Like doors, bridges are heavily symbolic in that they allow passage from one place to another. They were long associated with death, as the way by which the soul passed over into the next world – seen in the many legends from ancient civilisations around the world. It is also echoed in the superstition that it is dangerous for a funeral procession to take the corpse twice over the same bridge.

It is unlucky to be the first to cross a new bridge. If you part from a friend on or under a bridge, you will never meet again. It is unlucky to talk as you stand or walk under a bridge, while a modern version states it is unlucky to be under a bridge as a train passes over.

Graveyards Always places to be avoided for fear of what you might see or disturb, graveyards and graves had many taboos. To walk on a grave could be anything from disrespectful to dangerous (and if you shiver suddenly, it indicates someone is walking over the place where your grave will be). It is dangerous to disturb a grave, and worse still to rob it. Anyone using

bits of gravestones to build their house will bring death into the building, and if they are used on a road it will be plagued by accidents.

Graves were dug in an east–west direction; the Final Call on the Last Day would come from the Holy Land in the east, so the dead are buried with their feet in the east to sit up facing that direction on the day of resurrection. The holiest place to be buried was on the south side of a churchyard; the north was usually reserved for suicides and unbaptised children.

Rivers The most important river superstition is that no magic can be worked through them, so they were places of relative safety for fearful travellers. This belief was used by Robert Burns in *Tam o' Shanter*, his poem of Hallowe'en bewitching: the only way Tam can escape being dragged down to Hell by the witches is to ride his horse across the bridge over the river.

Trees There are as many tree superstitions as there are types of tree, but some are shared by trees in general. They were long thought sacred and the home of powerful spirits, so to touch or knock on wood was to pay them reverence and gain their help and protection. The connection of trees to the divine is universal across all cultures. The Egyptians believed gods lived in some trees; they were associated with the gods of Greece and Rome; the Buddha gained enlightenment as he meditated under a tree, and he was himself reincarnated as one 43 times. Trees feature throughout the Old Testament as sacred places, or fitting sites for

TOP 10 SUPERSTITIONS: 8

Touching or knocking on wood brings good luck

altars; and Christians believe humanity was condemned and redeemed through trees – the first, the tree of knowledge of good and evil in the Garden of Eden, and the second, the tree on which Christ died at Calvary.

This may have been one reason behind the draconian punishment of death for someone found cutting down a tree. Another old belief was that fairies lived either inside hollow trees or under their roots, so certain trees tended to be avoided. For more information on individual tree superstitions, see Plants p. 157.

THE SKIES

Few areas of experience show up human powerlessness so forcefully as the workings of the natural world and the elements – wind, sea and rain, the sun and the planets beyond.

A minute's reflection would convince most of us to include central heating and electric light somewhere in a top 10 of modern comforts. Their familiarity makes us forget what a difference they make in cossetting us from the outside world and all that is thrown about out there. With little more than candles to ward off the dark and a fire of logs or peat in the cold months, it was no wonder our ancestors devised rituals to praise the sun, charms to control the weather, and omens to foretell it.

The Sun

One of the twin supports of life, the sun was worshipped by the ancients for centuries. One of the earliest cults we know about was that of the Egyptian

sun-god Ra, dating back to 4000 years ago, and the straight sided pyramids the Egyptians built to entomb their dead pharaohs represented a solid model of a ray of sunlight pointing at the sky. Ra was the creator and he sailed across the sky by day, charting his boat through the Underworld at night.

Closer to home and dating from around the time of the pyramids is Stonehenge. Built to point at the rising sun of the summer solstice, it is thought to have been a sun temple or observatory. The fires that were lit across Britain at Beltane, Midsummer and Hallowe'en burned to strengthen the sun throughout the year.

SOME SUN SUPERSTITIONS

- a sun eclipse was a dread omen that foretold national disaster

- a baby born at sunrise would be lucky and successful; the opposite was true of one born as the sun went down

- happy the bride the sun shines on: for a bride to be hit by a shaft of sunlight on her wedding day was the best of omens

- a ray of sunlight falling on a funeral mourner was a death omen

Sun beliefs were so fundamental that they showed up in almost every culture and civilisation. Christianity adapted and grafted on a few, coinciding its ceremonies with the major events of the old pagan year. The sun itself was said to dance for joy in the sky as it rose each Easter Sunday morning and is always said to shine every Sunday, even if for just a few seconds.

The sun's direction was followed in all sorts of rites and ceremonies: east to west, left to right, sunwise or clockwise, and any kind of processions or movements – from dances, through churching processions to passing the after-dinner port – tend to follow this pattern. Any ceremony performed anti-sunwise (anti-clockwise) was usually done on purpose to summon the powers of Darkness.

The Moon

Like the sun, the moon was worshipped as a god by ancient people. It marked out the months and the passing of time, and with the sun, planets and stars, played an important part in governing human behaviour. It was vital in astrology, bringing in different influences as it crossed each zodiac sign and it was also linked with witchcraft.

The waxing (increasing) and waning (decreasing) of the moon was all-important, affecting not just the swell of tides but all earth's growing and changing things. But the most significant times in the moon's cycle were the new and the full moon.

New Moon It was very unlucky to see a new moon for the first time through glass or trees, and people often carried a silver coin with them to turn in their pocket when they caught sight of it. Pointing at it brought bad luck; safest of all was to bow or curtsey with a blessing – 'Yonder's the Moon, God save her

A WAXING MOON

- blood flow and blood pressure increased, so any blood-letting was never done then
- there was a greater risk during operations at this time, and an increased danger of infection
- seeds were planted then
- babies and animals born then were sure to thrive
- weddings were celebrated then to ensure a happy and fruitful marriage
- a death at this time would soon be followed by two more
- journeys and travel were best undertaken then

A WANING MOON

- growth was slowed, making this the best time for hair- and nail-cutting
- picking and harvesting were done then
- animals were not slaughtered then in case their meat would shrink
- animals born then would not thrive, and children would be unlucky
- this was the best time to move to a new house

Grace'. You could also make a wish on the new moon:

New moon, true moon, star in the stream,
Pray tell my fortune in my dream.

Full Moon The word 'lunatic' comes from the old Roman word for 'moon' and shows the very common idea that the mentally ill, idiots and other assorted afflicted were made worse by the full moon. Crime rates are often said to increase during the full moon. And many people not otherwise superstitious will make sure the curtains are closed so there is no danger of the moonlight shining on them as they sleep: the old superstitions say this will distort your face, make you crazy or, in some places, turn you into a werewolf.

The Stars

The souls of the dead or of slain warriors, the gods' dwelling place or the governors of events on earth, stars were looked on as heavenly, divine and magical things. Counting them or pointing at them was, as with the moon, disrespectful.

WISHING ON A STAR

Star light, star bright, first star I see tonight,
I wish I may, I wish I might
Have the wish I wish tonight.

Their magical association still lives on in popular beliefs about the wishing star, the first star seen in the evening. Your wish on a star would be granted, as long as it was kept secret. People still wish on shooting stars, although the wish must be made before the star disappears. In the past, shooting stars were thought to be souls coming to earth direct from heaven to be born. If the star appeared on your right side it was a good omen but bad luck was coming your way if it went past on your left.

Dog Days   Sirius, the Dog Star, rises with the sun from the first week in July until the second week in August; Romans called this period the Days of the Dog. Sirius was believed to add to the sun's heat to produce the hot and muggy days of late summer in the northern hemisphere and its influence was evil and varied:

- dogs went mad temporarily and were likely to attack humans
- it was an unhealthy period, with illness and disease prevalent: blood-letting was not advised and illnesses would last as long as the Dog Days
- insects and snakes proliferated and were more likely to sting and bite
- it was unhealthy to swim
- human behaviour was affected, and violence was more likely

ASTROLOGY

The most popular system of prediction today and followed at some time by almost everyone, even just by reading a newspaper horoscope. The positions of the sun, moon and planets are believed to exert their own particular influences on events and people on earth, and while potential can be determined and inferences drawn, astrology cannot foretell future events exactly.

Although astrology is over 4000 years old, the best known type that has survived to the present day is natal, or birth astrology. This uses a horoscope or birth chart that notes the planets' position at the time and place of birth to determine their influence on the subject's personality and future life. The most familiar part of a horoscope is the sun sign – the zodiac constellation that the sun was in at the subject's birth. These are the zodiac signs, or star signs, as they are usually called, that are so familiar to us (see opposite). Each sign has its own particular tendencies and qualities which are in turn influenced by the 10 planets:

- Sun
- Moon
- Mercury
- Venus
- Mars
- Jupiter
- Saturn
- Uranus
- Neptune
- Pluto

SIGNS OF THE ZODIAC

Aries 21 Mar–20 Apr
impulsive, innovative, independent

Taurus 21 Apr–21 May
stable, persevering

Gemini 22 May–22 Jun;
communicative, versatile, adaptable

Cancer 23 Jun–23 Jul
sensitive, protective, moody

Leo 24 Jul–23 Aug
aggressive, outgoing, confident, proud

Virgo 24 Aug–23 Sep
perfection-seeking, focused, discriminating

Libra 24 Sep–23 Oct
easy-going, affable, diplomatic, indecisive

Scorpio 24 Oct–22 Nov
intense, incisive, shrewd

Saggitarius 23 Nov–22 Dec
outgoing, enthusiastic, honest

Capricorn 23 Dec–19 Jan
conservative, inhibited, economical, dogged

Aquarius 20 Jan–19 Feb
inventive, selfless, eccentric

Pisces 20 Feb–20 Mar
intuitive, compassionate, enigmatic, dreamy

THE PLANETS

☉ **Sun** linked with personality
influences ego, leadership, creativity

☾ **Moon** linked with moods
influences feelings, fertility, cycles

☿ **Mercury** linked with thoughts
influences communication, versatility

♀ **Venus** linked with emotions
influences affections, morality, sociability

♂ **Mars** linked with activeness and drive
influences assertiveness, speed, energies

♃ **Jupiter** linked with expansion
influences optimism, benevolence, wellbeing

♄ **Saturn** linked with responsibility
influences discipline, wisdom, ambition, truth

♅ **Uranus** linked with change
influences originality, inventiveness, surprise

♆ **Neptune** linked with imagination
influences ideals, illusions, religions

♇ **Pluto** linked with depth and transformation
influences intensity, change

There are other astrological systems – the Chinese system, for example, uses the metaphor of animals rather than celestial bodies – but this is still the one most of us are most familiar with.

The Earth

One-time centre of the universe, Earth was also one of the four primal elements and the dust God used to mould human beings. It was always credited with special powers of healing and magic.

As already mentioned, Christ spread an earth-and-spittle poultice on the eyes of a blind man to cure him, and earth plasters and poultices were often used to treat illness. What worked best was earth from holy ground like a churchyard or where three lands met. Lying on the earth, in direct contact with it, also brought relief to the dying and those giving birth.

STORMS

For centuries storms were not just seen as bad omens but as displays of the gods' anger: Zeus, ruler of the Greek gods, had a habit of hurling bolts of lightning in his wrath. A storm was a sign of his

divine displeasure, and public meetings were instantly dispersed if a storm broke out. And Thor, Norse god of the sky, threw Mjolnir, the thunderbolt-hammer, about the sky.

In Britain storms were usually the Devil's work or that of witches, who summoned them up by whistling. The witches of North Berwick suffered a hard fate after conjuring up a storm to sink the ship bringing James VI of Scotland home from Norway. Church bells were often rung in a storm, as they were good against the storm-bringing demons of the air. Another belief was that a storm came as the sign of the death of a great man, or to fetch his soul. Plenty of examples, from Christ to Cromwell, fed this superstition.

The commonest storm superstition is that lightning never strikes the same place twice, but New York's Empire State building took 68 hits in one three-year period. Even more spectacular was the very unlucky US park ranger Roy C. Sullivan, hit by lightning seven times over a 35-year period. Anyone caught out in a storm might do well to remember this rhyme:

Beware of the oak,
It draws the stroke;
Avoid the ash,
It counts the flash;
Creep under the thorn,
It can save you from harm.

RAIN

> St Swithin's Day, if thou be fair
> For forty days twill rain nae mair,
> St Swithin's Day, if thou do rain,
> For forty days it will remain.

St Swithin Probably the best-known of all British rain superstitions is that of the 9th-century English St Swithin. Rain on his feast day, July 15th, is said to determine the weather for the next 40 days. The legend came from Swithin's wish to be buried not in an honoured spot inside his Winchester church but outside, next to the graves of the parish poor. One attempt by his followers to move his body inside the church on 15 July, 871 AD, was forced to halt by 40 days of relentless rain, and the legend of Swithin was born.

But not everyone was a believer, even in the superstitious 17th century:

If Swithin wept this year, the proverb says,
The weather will be foul for forty days.
But still exceptions to such rule there are,
As in this case (except some days be fair).
Husbandman ply thy work, no time mis-spending,
On Providence, not proverbs, still depending.

Beneficial Rain Of course, rain is a must for a successful harvest, and many rain rhymes and traditions have grown up around it, especially in country areas.

MAKING RAIN

- burning ferns
- scattering water on stones
- dipping a cross or saint's image in water

FORECASTING RAIN

- cows coming down off the hills
- cows raising their tails
- rheumatism twinges in sufferers
- aching corns on the feet

SYMBOLIC RAIN

- rain falling at a funeral shows the dead person's soul has reached heaven
- rain falling on a wedding party leaving the church was a good omen

HEALING RAIN

- rainwater that fell and was collected on Ascension Sunday, when Christ rose bodily into heaven, was credited with miraculous healing powers

RAIN RHYMES

Rain, rain, go away,
Come again another day.

Rain, rain, go to Spain
And never come here again.

RAINBOWS

Rainbow at night, sailor's delight;
Rainbow in the morning, sailor's warning;
Rainbow to windward, foul all the day;
Rainbow to leeward, damp runs away.

One of the oldest rainbow beliefs comes from the
book of Genesis, where the rainbow was a symbol of
God's promise after the Great Flood never again to
send rains to destroy the earth. Later, they came to
be seen as good omens. But the most familiar belief is
that there is a pot of gold at the point where a rainbow touches earth.

Rainbows are still thought magical and many people
make a wish when they see one. Almost every country
has its own rainbow superstition, but an idea common
almost everywhere in the past was that a rainbow
formed a bridge from earth to paradise, and that the
souls of the newly dead used it to cross over from one
world to the next. It is very disrespectful to point at a

rainbow and bad luck was bound to come to anyone who did – at the very least, the rain would come back on again.

WILDLIFE

The pre-industrial world, more closely in touch with
nature than we are, had an enormous range of animal
and bird superstitions.

Animals

Animals have always been credited with certain powers
and significance, giving rise to superstitions and
omens to explain away the unknown. There is probably more superstition and mythology attached to animals than any other branch of nature.

PET ANIMALS

Cat   Loved and hated almost equally, the cat is
almost an emblem of superstition and witchcraft. It
has been around humans a long time: 5000 years ago
cats were worshipped in Egypt and killing one was a
capital crime. If a family's cat died they went into
mourning, seeing it off with mummification and a full

TOP 10 SUPERSTITIONS: 5

Black cats are lucky,
especially if one crosses your path

Bast: the revered Egyptian mother-goddess was also known as Pasht, said to be the origin of the pet-name 'puss'

funeral procession complete with weeping. The cat's favourite toys were left in in its tomb for play in the afterlife.

The association of cats with sacredness continued with the Romans, who first introduced cats to Europe, but by the 17th century the circle had turned

CATS DON'T ...

- have nine lives
- suck away a baby's breath
- have eyes that shine in the dark (although, like the road markings, they do reflect the light)

ANIMALS   133

CAT LORE

- it is lucky if a black cat crosses your path, enters your house or comes on board your ship
- it is bad luck to kill a cat
- a cat leaving a sick person's house is a death omen, as is dreaming of a cat
- a bought cat will never be a good mouser
- a sick person is cured by washing them, throwing the water over the cat then chasing it out
- a storm is coming if a cat has its back to the fire

and the cat was infamous as a witch's familiar. In line with this belief, many animals were burned alive each year on Shrove Tuesday, before the start of Lent next day. This also protected a house against fire. Some other cat superstitions are shown above, but on behalf of cats some classic superstitions also need a bit of deflating (opposite).

Dog Despite its ever-faithful-friend image, many black omens are associated with this particular pet. These are just a few bad dog omens:

- a howling dog foretold death if someone was ill in a house
- a dog howling three times indicated someone had just died locally

- a whimpering dog foretold bad luck for its owners
- a dog running between friends foretold a falling-out
- a dog hiding under a table signalled stormy weather
- dreaming of a dog meant a friend was untrue

One particular type of dog was always feared – the black dog, a ghostly phantom that lived in deserted places: burial grounds, quiet roads, bridges and riversides. To see this dog foretold certain disaster, as in Suffolk in August, 1577, when a seemingly supernatural black dog appeared in Bungay parish church during a storm. It killed two worshippers and paralysed another, blasted the church clock's mechanism and left claw-marks on the door. The dog was also seen the same day at another church nearby. But the biggest fear

The black dog of Bungay, Suffolk: a contemporary account

came from 'mad' dogs, when Britain suffered the scourge of rabies: there were many superstitious cures for a mad dog's bite, from feeding the dog or its victim paper with charms written on, to feeding its victim pieces of the dog's cooked liver. These cures were still used in the late 19th century.

ANIMAL PARASITES

Bat Despite its modern-day protected status, this winged mouse-lookalike still has strong negative associations. As a black creature of the night it was associated with death, witchcraft and evil; Satan himself was often depicted as having bats' wings. And its more modern association with blood-sucking vampires has done little to revive the bat's reputation.

The old horror stories of bats becoming tangled up in long hair have been proved false, only to be replaced by a set of modern myths about the accuracy of bat 'radar' – yet bats still crash into things as they fly about. In the past, such collisions were taken as bad omens, of anything from rain to the death of someone in the house. Just as bad was if a bat flew into a room: the owner would have ill luck or illness, or would soon leave the property. Given most people's reluctance to share their homes with bats, even in less fastidious medieval times, this was an 'omen' that almost certainly grew up out of observed practice.

TOP 10 SUPERSTITIONS: 4

Rats will always desert a sinking ship

Rat The well-known rat-and-sinking-ship omen applies to houses and farms, too – ironically, abandonment by this parasite means ill-luck for those deserted.

In medieval times it was known that there was some connection between rats and bubonic plague, although no-one was quite sure what it was. But inevitably rats came to be omens of death. They were also thought susceptible to music and magical charms. Rat charmers have existed right up to the 20th century, with the most famous and dread example in Hamelyn, where the Pied Piper cleared the town first of rats, then of children, in 1284.

FARM ANIMALS

Cow In line with its benign nature, the cow is one animal with few negative associations. As one of the animals that shared the stable with the new-born Christ, the cow was regarded as particularly blessed: God gifted it with sweet breath for keeping the baby Jesus warm. And in some areas it is thought that every Christmas Eve cows still kneel down to adore the newborn Messiah.

But a couple of exceptions mar the cow's generally sweet-and-cuddly image. Cows breaking into an enclosed garden were seen as a bad omen, and a cow lowing in your face was a portent of anything from bad luck to death.

Donkey The coloured cross on the donkey's shoulders and back marks it out as an animal claimed by Christ from the time he rode into Jerusalem on one; the Holy Family was said to have escaped Herod by fleeing into Egypt on one, too. As a result of carrying these holy burdens, donkeys have been thought to have many healing and curative powers.

DONKEY CURES

- riding on a donkey while facing backwards towards its tail was a popular cure for many illnesses

- three hairs taken from a donkey's cross were prized in preventing illness when worn in a bag round the neck

- as a cure for whooping cough, sufferers were passed under a donkey, then over its back, three or nine times

- other infections, like scarlet fever, were cured by feeding the donkey some of the patient's hair

Goat In spite (or perhaps because) of being one of the stupidest farm animals, goats were associated with the Devil, and Satan himself was often depicted as a giant goat (*see p. 183*). Mimicking this, the leaders of witches' covens would wear a goat's head for certain ceremonies. One old belief stated that goats would always disappear for part of a day, as they all had to visit the Devil daily to have their beards combed.

Despite its demonic associations, goat beliefs were usually benign:

- meeting a goat at the start of a journey or business transaction was a good-luck omen
- goats kept in a stable protected horses from harm
- a goat's horn under your pillow would cure insomnia

Horse The importance of horses in almost every area of life in the pre-industrial world made them synonymous with speed and power. Witches and fairies could enchant them and

many charms, including horse brasses, were hung around the stable to protect them. Plaiting a horse's tail with ribbons, too, warded off evil. Some humans, notably horse-whisperers, had an uncanny understanding with them.

Like some other animals, especially dogs, they seemed to sense death and unbodied presences that humans were unaware of. White horses were particularly significant – lucky in some areas, unlucky in others. Horses' bones were thought to protect against evil, so they were often built into house walls. They were also a fertility symbol: hence the importance of the hobby horse in traditional Mayday celebrations.

Pig Once a sacred animal for many, including the Norse and Celtic people. Its high status meant some people still avoided pig-meat long after the original reason was forgotten – although in hot countries with no means of keeping meat fresh, the parasite pigs carry provided one very good reason for not eating pork.

Pigs were said to see the wind, and if a pig carried straw in its mouth a storm was brewing. Anything to do with pigs was bad luck to sailors – even mentioning them could be enough to turn a boat back to port.

Sheep As with most other farm animals, sheep were useful weather barometers: sheep lying down is a good sign, but restless and noisy sheep foretell bad weather. They were also used in the cure of various ailments and illnesses. An adder-bite on a human was bad news for any nearby sheep, which could expect to be slaughtered and skinned on the instant so the victim could be wrapped in its skin, thus saving their life. And, contrary to the frustrating norm of sheep-blocking-the-road hold-ups, it was very good luck to meet a flock of sheep while you were on a journey.

But sheep superstitions were insignificant compared to the importance of the lamb as an icon. It always signified innocence and purity and was for centuries sacrificed to various gods. It became the icon of Christ and it is said that on Easter Sunday at sunrise anyone climbing to the top of a hill will see, in the sun's centre, the image of the Lamb of God: the lamb, bearing a flag with a red cross. No witch or demon could ever take on the shape of a lamb in their magic.

The Lamb and Flag

The first lamb seen in spring is a good omen, especially if it is black, but its head must be turned towards you; if it is looking the other way, bad luck will follow.

OTHER ANIMALS

Fox One of the animals witches could change into. A fox coming near or into a house was a death omen. To see a single fox brought good luck but seeing more than one did not. In parts of Europe, people wore fox tongues as amulets, in the hope that the fox's cunning and boldness would be transferred to them.

Frog & Toad Unlucky in that they always seemed on the receiving end of any casual cruelty being meted out to animals. They had a place in various charms and magic, especially healing, where they were used to treat all kinds of malady from imagined to serious. All the remedies seemed to involve either swallowing live frogs or imprisoning toads until they wasted away. Other, ill-wishing charms to make people suffer called for frogs to be impaled on something spiky – pins, needles or thorns – to produce the same suffering in the victim. And although its involvement in witchcraft as a familiar gave the toad less of a victim status, toads also had a rough time. It was thought lucky to meet one, although given its all-round usefulness, we have to wonder just who the meeting was lucky for.

Hare Once worshipped in Britain at one time as a symbol of fertility and spring, hares' associations with power continued on into witchcraft, as they were one of the animals a witch could turn into. Like a were-wolf, the favoured method of despatch for them was a silver bullet. Hares were thought to bring bad luck generally, but some situations were even worse:

- it was a black omen if a hare crossed your path at the start of a journey or new venture, like a wedding

- if a pregnant woman saw a hare her baby would have a hare lip (tearing her petticoat would avert it)

- to dream of a hare was an omen of death

Some fairly quirky ideas existed, including the one of the hermaphrodite hare, said to swap sexes yearly.

Hedgehog Eaten to cure fits and killed by farmers for drinking cows' milk as they slept, it was no wonder hedgehogs were thought unlucky. But they were valued as forecasters. They were said to stop hibernating on February 2nd (Candlemas Day) to see if winter was over. If so, they stayed out, but if they returned to their dens, another six weeks' bad weather was due.

Mole Yet another small animal dissected in the name of quack medicine. Its foot prevented toothache and rheumatism, its skin was used as a type of poultice and its blood washed away warts. The moles' revenge may have been to dig hills in people's gardens: one of these appearing in a previously molehill-free area foretold the death of someone in the house.

Rabbit One very popular luck-bringing superstition was to say Rabbits or White Rabbits when you got out of bed on the first day of each month. Many hare-related superstitions also applied to rabbits as, for example, in the case of the egg-bringing Easter Hare whose place has now been taken by the Easter Bunny.

Seal Seals had a powerful grip on the imagination
of coastal communities. Especially in Scotland, legends of the selkie, who left the sea to become human,
were strong. Selkies were very beautiful and if their
shed seal skin could be captured by a human and hidden, they were forced to stay on the land in human
form. But myth and natural justice always warned that
the selkie would discover their skin at some point and
take to the water again, leaving wife, husband, children or any other human attachment, never to be seen
again.

Snake The adder, Britain's only poisonous snake,
was a creature feared not just for its bite but also
because it was ill-omened. It was very bad luck to see
one and not kill it. Its bite could be treated with fried
adder fat taken from a snake freshly killed for the purpose; other remedies included holding a bird against
the bite, making a poultice of herbs and saying
charms.

Birds

Their gift of flight has given birds a special place in
belief, as messengers between heaven and earth, as
angels, or as the souls of the dead ascending to heaven.
Many birds of ill-omen have in common the fact that
they are birds of prey – a classification dating back to
Moses, who classified birds as clean or unclean.

BIRD BELIEFS

- every culture has bird superstitions, where they are gods, their messengers, or the souls of heroes

- in ancient Rome the College of Augurs divined bird movement and behaviour to see omens of future events

- the direction of a bird's call is an omen: from the north expect bad news or a bad event; the west, good luck; the east, love; and the south, a good harvest

- a bird landing on the windowsill, tapping at the window pane or flying in the window are all death omens

- it is unlucky to see a flock of birds as you set out on a journey, or to see a bird of night, by day

Many individual types have their own particular place in legends, superstitions, omens and lore.

SEABIRDS AND WATERBIRDS

Most birds that live on or near water, according to old belief, are the souls of the dead and bad luck will come to anyone who harms one.

Albatross The *Rhyme of the Ancient Mariner* featured the ancient belief that to kill an albatross brings bad luck to a ship and all aboard. Like other seabirds, an albatross following a ship has always been seen as the soul of a dead sailor wanting to stay near his old ship.

Heron Waterbirds also have a share of superstitious lore. From ancient times the heron was a bird of good omen, symbolising rebirth to the ancient Egyptians. But in other countries, especially in Scotland, a single heron is an omen of death; the writer DK Broster wove her *Flight of the Heron* historical-thriller trilogy around this superstition. And the curlew, with its eerie, human-like call, is also unlucky, foreshadowing anything from a storm at sea to a death.

Kingfisher One of the birds Noah let out of the Ark, the kingfisher flew so high the sun singed its breast feathers and its plumage took on the sky's blue. For centuries kingfishers were associated with calm seas. From Greek legend, the 14 days around the Winter Solstice, when kingfishers nested, was a period of storm-free calm: these were the first halcyon days.

Seagull Like the albatross, respected by sailors. Three gulls flying overhead omens the death of the watcher or someone close to them.

Swan This is the bird of omen and superstition *par excellence*, featuring in ancient myth from Scandinavia and Siberia to ancient Greece and Rome. The swan's great beauty has always made it an object of mystery

Threatening omens of doom and disaster – not to mention powerful wings and a tendency to bite – have helped keep swans safe through the ages

and, sometimes, hostility. Possibly because of this, the notion has grown up that an early death will come to a swan-killer, usually within a year. The swan was also a good-luck omen to sailors who used it as a figurehead, as it never dives fully below the waves. Some believed the swan was a shape-shifter that took on human form, like the selkie or seal. An enduring belief from the time of ancient Greeks, and mentioned by Shakespeare, is that swans sing just before they die, calling out their joy at returning to the god whose messengers they are. Long-held country beliefs also had it that swans laid their eggs during thunderstorms and that it took a crack of lightning to hatch the young.

BIRDS OF NIGHT

Owl Owls sit uncomfortably in any division of birds of good and bad omen, at once representing wisdom, darkness and death: for example, dreaming of an owl can mean you need advice from an older person, or it can omen death. Owls were traditional witches' familiars, perhaps for their nocturnal habits and their wisdom.

An owl landing on the roof omened death in a house and it was almost as bad luck to see one or hear one screech by day. Potions were made from owls and owl-eggs because of its status as a bird of wisdom. These treated 'mental' illness such as alcholism, epilepsy, rabies or madness.

The solitary bird of night, of wisdom and of darkness

Nightingale This nocturnal bird never had any dark associations. It was thought melancholy in ancient times, but Christians reinterpreted it as the soul in darkness anticipating the return of the lord of light with such joy that it could not be silent.

BIRDS OF PREY

All members of the crow family – rooks, ravens, jackdaws and magpies – share to some extent the ill-luck and general bad vibes associated with their kin. But each also had its own particular superstitions.

Jackdaw The two-tone jackdaw, with all the dualities its colouring suggested, was looked on with suspicion. It was unlucky to see one, especially to the left, and if one landed on your roof a death was imminent.

Magpie The now-commoner magpie shares some superstitions with the jackdaw and, like it, is also two coloured: dark and light, bad and good. Everyone knows a magpie-counting rhyme, although the numbers' meaning varied from place to place. The rhymes show the ambivalent attitudes to the bird (*see p. 150*). Someone setting out on a journey might be unsettled at the sight of a magpie, but whether it was good or bad depended on the direction it came from. Tame magpies were kept as watch-birds – they began chattering when anyone approached the house. It was this harsh, noisy call that, by legend, led to Noah's banishing the bird from Ark to sit out on the roof.

MAGPIES IN VERSE

One for sorrow, two for joy,
Three for a girl, four for a boy,
Five for silver, six for gold,
Seven is a secret never to be told.

Clean birds by sevens, unclean by twos,
The dove of the heavens is the bird I choose.

One sorrow, two mirth,
Three a wedding, four a birth,
Five Heaven, six Hell,
Seven is the De'il's ain sel'(f).

Raven One of the most symbolic of birds. Messenger of the Norse god Odin, it was borne as a symbol on the banners of Viking invaders – possibly the source of its first association with evil. On the other hand it was also associated with British hero-king Arthur. Like most rooks, the raven has its good omens: it is lucky to meet one (but not two; three is even worse), although a croaking raven is not good, especially with a sick person nearby. But the best-known of Britain's raven superstitions is undoubtedly that of the ravens of the Tower of London: if these birds leave, legend states that the Crown, and Britain, will fall. But as the raven inmates have their wings clipped to make sure they stay in hopping distance, the odds are loaded pretty heavily against this catastrophe.

Mean, moody and magical: the Tower's ravens

Rook The gregarious, noisy, family-dwelling rook was never held in dread. But bad luck would be sure to follow for a family if a rook colony deserted a rookery at their house or land. And some farmers also saw rooks' nests as aerial barometers: if nests were high in the trees the coming summer would be warm, but nests built lower down forecast a wet, windy season.

DOMESTICATED BIRDS

Cockerel The cockerel that crows to greet the dawn has always been important in symbolism. As herald of the day it was laden with religious significance for the Egyptians, the ancient Greeks and Christians, who saw it as a guardian against the forces of darkness and evil.

Cockerels performed this symbolic duty as weather-vanes on church spires, turning in all directions to look out for evil and keeping watch by night when church bells were silent. It spied out the shame of St Peter in his denial of Christ, it was the first creature to proclaim Christ's birth on the first Christmas Day, and will crow on the Last Day to warn the living and awaken the dead to Judgement. It is a powerful symbol of resurrection.

A white cock was lucky as it brought protection to the house where it lived. A black one, on the other hand, was associated with black magic, witchcraft and the Devil, and was often used in ritual sacrifice.

Hen Apparently hardly interesting enough to have any superstitious interest. A hen bold enough to crow like a cock was a bad omen, and would soon be killed.

OTHER BIRDS

Of the many other birds that feature in traditional belief, a few that stand out as having more than the usual amount of superstitious lore attached to them.

Cuckoo

- late spring cuckoo song was a good omen for crops; early song meant frost and a poor harvest
- hearing a cuckoo was lucky, if you turned over a coin in your pocket and made a wish

Dove

- their status as emblems of peace comes from the Book of Genesis; the return to the Ark of a dove with an olive leaf in its beak symbolised the flood's end and God's peace with the world
- no-one can die on a dove-feather bed or pillow

Eagle

- highest of the birds, signifying bravery, strength, authority and spiritual power
- audible eagle cry heralded a great event
- bad luck would dog the robber of an eagle's nest

Robin

- friendly to humans, its red breast came from pulling a thorn out of Christ's head
- it is bad luck to harm a robin or touch its nest

Swallow

- it was lucky if a swallow nested in your house but the luck would turn if the nest were destroyed
- an old recipe for swallow soup claimed to cure a range of serious neurological disorders

Insects

Spiders   Not an insect, strictly speaking, spiders are the luckiest of creepy-crawlies – doubly so, as it brings bad luck to kill them, no matter how big and scary they are. To have a spider living in your house meant good luck and happiness would be yours, and if one dropped down from the ceiling it signalled money was coming your way. Some money spiders (often small, red ones) also brought special financial rewards. Spiders also featured in many primitive medicinal cures, most of which involved imprisoning a spider in a box or bag until it died, taking your particular disease away with it.

Beetles   Beetles were bad-luck omens, especially if found inside a house. Worse was if a beetle ran over someone's shoe – death was coming. Another dread death omen was the eerie, seemingly inexplicable tapping of a death-watch beetle. But a householder couldn't even enjoy the satisfaction of despatching it: a beetle-killer could expect anything from bad weather to personal bad luck.

Bees   Sources of food and drink and models of order and industry, bees have been respected since ancient times. They were called messengers of the gods and in some places were even seen as holy – bees' wax was made into church candles. Even the sight of a

BEE RHYME

A swarm of bees in May is worth a load of hay,
A swarm of bees in June is worth a silver spoon,
A swarm of bees in July is not worth a fly.

swarm was always a good omen. With so many positive associations, you could only expect bad luck if you killed one. A bee landing on you was the sign of a blessing, and you were not allowed to flick it away.

An almost mystic bond was said to exist between bees and their keeper; to make sure the bees stayed happy, keepers told them all the household and local events and gossip. And if the keeper died, the bees had to be told immediately, or else they would fly away. Bees' stings were (and still are) a cure for rheumatism and joint disorders – diseases that their often-stung keepers were said not to suffer from.

Lice & Fleas In the days when personal hygiene was a far less important consideration than now, lice infestation was common, although always unwelcome. A new infestation on someone previously clean was a sign they had been cursed by a witch. And the finding of a single louse was thought to be an omen of death. Even for those who had been infested, becoming clean was little comfort: lice or fleas deserting a previously infested host was a sure sign of the person's imminent death. One way to stay flea-free was, not surprisingly, by being clean: sweeping the doors, windows and all cracks of the home on 1st March, the start of spring, would keep the fleas out of the house for the year to come.

PLANTS

Plants had a central place in folk-medicine, charms and enchantments, and there are plenty of superstitions relating to all types. Some of the more common and more typical ones are detailed here.

Trees

Bay The old superstition that a withered bay tree foreshadows a death in the family makes an appearance in Shakespeare, but bays were auspicious long before then. The Greeks held it sacred for its healing powers and as a protection against evil. It was widely used in Christmas decoration as well as in funerals, when its apparent regenerative powers were a sign of hope and resurrection for the mourners. These are a few more bay superstitions:

- a bay planted near a house wards off the plague
- bay leaves carried about protect against evil
- bay leaves under your pillow give sweet dreams
- lightning never strikes a bay tree

Hawthorn This was another tree sacred to the ancients, and then revered by Christians as the tree used to make Christ's crown of thorns. It was treated with great respect generally. There were strong associations with magic and the suspicious-minded tended to keep away from hawthorn trees on days like Hallowe'en and Midsummer's Eve. And dire warnings meant all but the most brave or foolish were content to let a hawthorn grow in their garden.

Oak   Sacred to pre-Christian people, the oak was renowned as the tree most likely to be hit by lightning in a storm. Acorns from the oak were often kept on windowsills to act as lightning deflectors. The oak was a symbol of strength in perseverance in its long, slow growth from an acorn: Great Oaks from Little Acorns Grow, went the saying.

Couples were married under traditional marriage-oaks, and the Christian church also adopted the tree: many gospel-oaks were planted to mark out parish boundaries. Pieces of the wood cured various ailments

Autumn leaves:
the oak has a long-revered
tradition in Britain

when rubbed on afflicted areas and women who embraced an oak tree were guaranteed a virile and fruitful husband. Oak leaves and twigs became a royalist symbol after Charles II was saved in the wake of the disastrous Battle of Worcester by hiding in an oak tree.

Rowan

The most effective protection against witches, fairies or any type of ill-wishing. Its wood was used in house building for protection, babies' cradles were made from it, sprigs were worn as protective decorations and tools around the farm were made from it to ward off any bewitchment. Its berries, too, were worn or fed to the animals.

Willow Sprigs of willow used to be sent maliciously to jilted lovers whose sweethearts married someone else; the 'weeping willow' was a symbol of grieving and lost love, and was often planted in graveyards.

Yew Another tree planted in graveyards and churchyards, the yew's great longevity associated it with eternal life, and sprigs were often carried by mourners and put in coffins, symbolising the continuation of life beyond death. But bad luck followed if a yew branch were brought into the house, as it would come to anyone who harmed the tree.

Flowers

An enormous number of superstitions are attached to flowers, both specifically and in general, and their meanings were symbolic: for example, the bridal tradition of carrying orange blossom to a wedding symbolised growth and fertility, as the orange blooms and bears fruit all year. Such meanings were centuries-old but by Victorian times the practice had developed into a whole unspoken language with each flower and the way it was presented revealing an emotion, association or even a specific sentence. There are too many to list all, but the charts that follow show some of the commonest.

SAY IT WITH FLOWERS

almond blossom	sweetness, delicacy
anemone	withered hopes, forsaken
azalea	temperance
bluebell	constant kindness
buttercup	ingratitude
carnation	betrothal, marriage, eternal love
striped	refusal
chrysanthemum	declaration of love
cornflower	delicacy
crocus	do not abuse
daffodil	regard
daisy	innocence
dead leaves	melancholy
fern	sincerity
forget-me-not	true love
geranium	recalling a meeting
holly	foresight
hyacinth	playfulness
iris	I have a message for you
lavender	distrust
lilac	humility

SAY IT AGAIN WITH FLOWERS

lily	falsehood
lily of the valley	return of happiness
magnolia	love of nature
marigold	pain, anger, jealousy
mistletoe	overcome all obstacles
narcissus	egotism
peony	shame
poppy	fading pleasures, consolation
primrose	early youth
rhododendron	danger
rose	love, beauty
red	declaration of love
white	silence
yellow	unfaithfulness, jealousy
shamrock	Ireland, lightheartedness
snowdrop	purity, innocence, strength
sunflower	adoration
sweet pea	delicate pleasure, departure
tulip	fame
violet	faithfulness in love
wildflower	fidelity in misfortune

Other Plants

Medicines, flavourings, perfumes, preservatives, poisons, witch-repellents – the list of plant uses was almost endless, and many plant traditions and superstitions flourished.

Clover One of the best-known luck bringers of all is the four-leafed clover (*see p. 90*) but the normal, three-leafed variety also has plenty of supersitious associations. A clover's three leaves were said to represent the Trinity – Father, Son and Holy Spirit – so its religious associations helped to ward off evil. Not only did it always bring good luck to its wearer, but until relatively recently people used it to help them see fairies. On the medicinal side, clover infusions were used to help treat skin diseases. Five-leafed clovers weren't so lucky, causing illness unless the finder gave them away instantly.

Dandelion Widely regarded as a weed although it is, strictly speaking, a flower. Its diuretic properties have long been celebrated by children in its nickname, 'pee-the-bed'. Not surprisingly, dandelion tea is generally thought good for the liver and kidneys. Children use dandelion clocks to tell the time, with the number of puffs it takes to blow away the seeds indicating the hour. Young women also used the method to tell them how many years they would wait to get a husband.

Hemlock   Synonymous with poisons and witches' evil brews, hemlock generally had a bad press in the annals of plant lore. Although poisonous in its undiluted form, it was widely used in infusions, poultices and other folk-medicinal mixtures to treat various ills, including gout and rheumatism.

Holly   A winter decoration long before Christianity. For the Romans it was a symbol of friendship and goodwill, and elsewhere it was hung on doors for luck and to repel witches. Christianity later claimed it: Christ's crown of thorns was sometimes said to be holly, and the once-yellow berries were reddened by his blood. Traditionally, holly is not brought into the house until Christmas Eve or it will start quarrels, and it must be burned after the 12-day celebration; another version says it is bad luck to burn any holly still green.

Ivy   Holly's decorative partner at midwinter, ivy was one of the evergreens used to ensure the return of the spring. A Roman ivy-berry infusion dispelled the effects of a hard night's drinking, and an ivy-leaf tea soothed a hangover. Ivy growing on a house protected it from evil, but if it withered the house would pass to others. Ivy given as a gift is said to break up a friendship.

It was also used in divination and in medicine, with various soaked leaves and infusions helping to cure skin complaints, runny noses, corns and sore eyes.

Juniper   A plant associated with protection, a meaning it also carries in the language of flowers. A juniper bush was a hiding-place from Herod's troops for the Baby Jesus. Smoke from burned juniper wood was traditionally said to keep away evil spirits, and juniper fires were also burned to keep out the plague.

Mandrake   The mandrake's human-looking root with open legs have seen it associated with fertility and potency since ancient times. Mandrake-root solution was drunk as an aphrodisiac and bits of it were

'Pictures' of female and male mandrake roots

carried about as love-charms. It was used it as a hallucinogen by seers to bring on visions; as an analgesic to relieve pain; in liquid as a sleeping potion; and, chewed, as an anaesthetic before operations. It had to be used carefully, though, as too much brought on dementia and madness. Getting one out of the ground was not easy, as it was said to scream enough to drive hearers mad as it was pulled up, and there was a host of convoluted rules for gathering it. It had to be kept under special conditions, too, but once someone had one they could expect to be not just richer but more fertile; hardly surprising that some people risked being denounced as witches just to get hold of some.

Mistletoe The best known of all mistletoe customs is to kiss under it at Christmas. It was held sacred by the Celts and the Norse, for whom it was a plant of peace – a possible source of the Christmas-time kiss ritual. The Druids reverently cut it for ceremonies at the Midsummer and Midwinter solstices, and its strong pagan associations have seen it barred from most church decorations at Christmas. The plant grows as a parasite on trees, but mistletoe grown on an oak had special magical properties. To cut down a mistletoe-bearing tree was to invite death and destruction.

Nightshade Plants in the nightshade family were all believed to have magical powers. Most famous is deadly nightshade, belladonna: poisonous in large amounts, it was used as a hallucinogen by seers and those who wanted to see spirits. It was also an ingredient in witches' flying ointment. But worn around the neck of a person or animal, woody nightshade protected against spells and the Evil Eye.

Parsley   Very unlucky associations surround this herb even though it is so useful in cooking. Ancient Greeks and Romans used it as a graveside plant – one of its many death associations. To prevent a death in the gardener's family it must only be sown on Good Friday, although some traditions warned against having it in the garden at all. 'Parsley grows better for a wicked man than a good one' was another proverb and to transplant it was also a dangerous practice that could result in bad luck at best, death at worst. Despite its death-dealing reputation, parsley was quite widely used not just in the kitchen but for medicinal purposes, in everything from a poisons antidote through a hair restorer to the ubiquitous rheumatism cure.

Rosemary   Representing remembrance in the language of flowers, rosemary had associations with the Holy Family and was a revered plant. It was used in wedding and funeral ceremonies – sprigs were dropped into the grave to signify the deceased would not be forgotten. In medicine it was used for nervous disorders, and gave protection against evil spells and ill-wishing. Rosemary was said only to flourish for the righteous and for a mistress who ruled both her husband and her house.

Rue   Literally synonymous with repentance, though not all its associated superstitions are negative. Rue is said to grow better if it has been stolen from someone else's garden and it also had great power against evil. Used in nosegays it warded off both evil spirits and the plague and it also worked as an antidote to poison. Infused rue treated convulsions, fits and even rabies, when a paste of rue leaves was also applied to the bite.

Sage   Sage shares many beliefs and associations with rosemary, but instead of remembrance this plant represents wisdom. Sage featured in folk-medicine healing sore throats, sharpening the eyesight, improving the memory and cleaning teeth, and its all-round usefulness was enhanced by its use in marriage-divinations: 12 sage leaves plucked in time with the striking clock at midnight on Midsummer's Eve would reveal the picker's spouse-to-be behind them.

Thyme   Thyme was associated in ancient superstition with the ghosts of the murdered, and its scent was strongest at the site of past murders. The souls of the dead were supposed to live in thyme-flowers. Medicinally, the plant featured in prescriptions for treatments for depression.

FOOD & DRINK

Certain types of foods were more important in the world of superstitions than others – some, like eating Hot Cross Buns on Good Friday, are still well-known to us today but others, like the old custom of nut-throwing at weddings, have been virtually forgotten.

APPLE SAYINGS

An apple a day keeps the doctor away

One bad apple spoils the whole crop

To eat an apple without rubbing it first is to challenge the Devil

---

Apples The best-known apple story may not actually have featured an apple at all. The fruit Eve ate in Eden, supposed by everyone to have been an apple, was simply the fruit of the tree of knowledge. But apples were associated with the gods elsewhere and often crop up in ancient legends as a magical fruit.

Apples also featured in autumn and winter customs. One Christmas-time ceremony was apple-wassailing, where the health of the apple tree was drunk by a crowd of noisy, cider-swilling revellers. Ducking for apples is a party game for Hallowe'en, and apples also featured in various spouse-divining games at that bewitched time: a strip of peeled apple skin flung over your left shoulder would land in the shape of your future spouse's initial. Apples were widely used in beauty preparations, as health drinks, face packs and wart removers.

Beans An auspicious food all round, and strongly connected with death. The Egyptians said they were sacred and would not eat them, and Greek mathematician Pythagoras thought the souls of the dead lived in them (he died, so legend has it, because he wouldn't run across a field of beans to flee his attackers). More recent beliefs in a similar vein state that souls of the dead lived in bean-plant flowers and their strong scent would bring on hallucinations, confusion, nightmares and even madness. The Romans thought ghosts threw beans at their houses at night to bring the inhabitants bad luck and as a result, they devised bean-burning ceremonies at gravesides to placate the spirits.

Very specific advice was given on when beans should

be planted but if one bean in a row came up white, death was predicted in their planter's family. But every leap year, broad-bean growers expected their beans to grow the wrong way up.

Blackberries Blackberries are strongly connected with the Devil. Lucifer fell into a blackberry bush when he was thrown out of Heaven and their colour was said to come from his spittle, his hot breath or, more lavatorially, his having wiped his tail on them. He repeated the exercise at a certain date every year, resulting in a taboo on picking later-fruiting berries.

Bread The single most revered food in wheat-growing areas, the 'staff of life' has always been surrounded by custom and superstition. From the pagan Corn Spirit through to Christ's changing of bread into his body at the Last Supper and its remembrance in the

Eucharist, bread has long held a central place in religious belief. Some bread beliefs are listed on page 172.

BREAD BELIEFS

- the sign of the cross should be made over dough as it rises to protect it from evil spirits

- if baking bread overflows its tin, illness is omened in the family

- only one person must put the bread in the oven; if two people do it, they will quarrel

- a hole in the centre of a baked loaf suggested a death in the family within the year

- it is bad luck to cut a loaf from both ends

- arguments in the family will follow if bread crumbles when it is cut

- a loaf turned upside down meant illness in the family or the loss of a ship at sea

- it is bad luck to take the last slice from a plate but if it is offered and accepted, wealth and happiness follow

- bread baked on Good Friday and Christmas Eve had special healing powers

- babies about to be christened were often given a gift of bread and butter for luck

- if two people reach for the same piece of bread, a visitor is coming

- throwing away bread was always frowned on; whoever did so would go hungry later in life

Eggs The best-known egg superstitions we still have today are probably those of Easter Eggs, but there are many more relating to mundane, everyday eggs. Yokeless eggs presaged unhappiness and very small eggs were an omen of death, as were double-yolkers. Breaking eggshells over a child protected it from the Evil Eye and it was also thought that witches could sail in an eggshell; many people poked a spoon through the upturned bottom of their empty boiled-egg shell to put a stop to such carry-on. Eggs should not be brought into a house after dark, or on a Sunday. Every major religion had an egg superstition – often a centrally important one. Eggs were used in magic spells for good and ill, and in healing processes.

Fish Like the egg, the fish plays a large part in the symbolism of the major religions. In fact, it has become a symbol of a Christian (now commonly displayed on the little fish-icon bumper stickers), indicating that the person has been caught by the 'fisher of men'.

Fishermen also had their own set of beliefs:

- you must throw back the first fish you catch; this used to be as a payment to the god of the sea

- but if you lose the first fish you catch then your entire trip will be unsuccessful

- if you count the fish you've caught, you won't catch any more on that trip

Eating fish was supposed to make you more intelligent and for good luck you had to eat it from head down to tail. Fish were used in folk remedies. The benefits of fish oils are well known now and in the past they were used to treat skin conditions. Less scientifically proven as a cure for whooping-cough was for the patient to hold a disembodied trout-head in their mouth.

Hot Cross Buns   Another Christian graft-on to an older pagan Spring custom. Buns baked on Good Friday morning were said not just to have healing properties but to keep fresh for the entire year. Sailors took them to sea to prevent shipwrecks.

Milk   The old consolation, 'There's no use crying over spilt milk' didn't have much to do with superstitious practice; spilling some milk on the ground was lucky, as it left a gift for the fairies which they would reward. But this was one of the few exceptions allowed in the waste of what was seen as a pure food.

*A lucky gift for
some thirsty fairies*

Most milk superstitions
were designed to make sure your cows stayed good
milkers:

- the first-ever milk from a cow was put in a bronze
  bowl to make sure she stayed prolific
- hairs were pulled from the tail of a cow that was sold
  to make sure she stayed a good milker
- stepping in the milk bucket would dry up your cows
- milk was sold with a pinch of salt added so the cow
  that gave it could not be bewitched

Nuts Synonymous with fruitfulness, nuts were
associated with love, fertility and childbearing. The
French pelted newlyweds with them; the more
reserved Romans presented them. For the Germans,
'going a-nutting' was a Carry-On style sex slang and in
some places a good nut crop on the local trees
omened the arrival of a healthy number of babies
within the year. Like other fruits of autumn, nuts were

used in Hallowe'en divination; a young woman would put two nuts in the fire, representing herself and her lover. If they burned together the omens were good but if they rolled apart or didn't burn at all, the love was doomed.

Onions   The onion was an all-round performer, with uses in areas as diverse as cooking, folk-medicine and witch-repellents, where it was used as an antidote to witchcraft. Its effects were varied and quite different on different people: some thought it an aphrodisiac; warrior-king Alexander the Great believed it heightened his troops' aggression and encouraged them to eat it before battle; and Indian gurus said it induced tranquillity.

Just to have some in the house was a protection against witchcraft and leaving a cut onion in the house acted as a germ magnet, thus sparing the inhabitants any diseases that were flying about. Boiled onion and vinegar was a hangover cure (what that did to a delicate stomach can only be imagined) while a salted onion rubbed on the skin cures chilblains. Finally, onions were also edible weather-forecasters:

> *Onion skin very thin,*
> *Mild winter coming in.*
> *Onion skin thick and tough,*
> *Coming winter very rough.*

Oranges   The prolific orange plant is a fertility symbol, and both fruit and flowers are a symbol of love and fruitfulness between lovers. For this reason the blossom of the orange was a traditional feature of any bridal bouquet, ensuring the marriage would not be a childless one.

Peas   A pod with one pea in it is a good-luck omen; better still is a nine-pea pod. If you throw it over your shoulder and make a wish, your wish is guaranteed to come true. A woman who opened a nine-pea pod could put the pod over her door, and the next man to come in would be her future husband. The same pod could also be used as a rub-on cure for warts – probably a far more useful help when it came to attracting a husband.

Salt   Not always the common, taken-for-granted commodity it is now, salt was expensive, difficult to extract, precious and heavily laden with symbolism and superstition. It was used as a preservative, so came to symbolise life and a lack of decay. On the other hand, it was also sterile and associated with barrenness. Its high price meant visitors were honoured to receive it, so it became a sign of hospitality, trust and friendship. Soldiers in ancient Rome might be paid in salt, so precious it became a substitute currency; from this practice arose the expression that a person was 'not worth his salt'. These were some other beliefs associated with it:

SALT SUPERSTITIONS

- a pinch of salt was left in a baby's cradle to protect it until it was christened
- wearing a small bag of salt around your neck protected you from the Evil Eye
- salt was thrown on the threshold of a new house for luck
- salt was an unlucky word for sailors and must never be mentioned at sea

Of course, the best known of all salt superstitions was the taboo against spilling it – a very bad omen.

- if the salt was spilled in a particular person's direction, bad luck was coming to that person
- spilled salt should not be swept up but thrown over the left shoulder (into the face of the Devil)
- enough tears must be cried to dissolve away the spilled salt

Tea Most tea superstitions concern prediction from tea-leaves, but there are some other tea beliefs. If two people pour tea from the same pot, both will have bad luck. A teapot without its lid is also an ill omen, and to stir the tea in the pot will cause an argument.

Anyone wanting their tea-cup read should drink their tea, swirl the leaves left in the cup around three times then turn it upside-down on the saucer to drain it. Shapes that suggested themselves in the leaves were symbolic representations of what the future had in store for the drinker. For example, a hand indicated friendship, a pair of scissors, argument and separation. Their position in the cup indicated when the events would happen – near the rim, and the incident could be expected soon – and the number of leaves indicated the general state of the person's life: so someone with many large leaves might enjoy a rich, full life. Tea-leaf reading could also be practised with coffee grinds or any other drink that left sediment in the bottom of the cup.

THE SUPERNATURAL

In the pre-scientific world, everything was related to
the supernatural to some degree . The spiritual was an
everyday part of the world and made itself evident in
many, often terrifying ways, with evil and danger
lurking unsuspected and waiting to pounce at any
opportunity.

Magic

There was hardly anyone, especially in the distant
past, who didn't believe that the supernatural could
be summoned and that some people could bring
about change in un-natural ways, just by willing it.
This could range from the neo-religious high magic of
groups like alchemists or the Rosicrucians, to the
everyday folk-magic, charms, potions and curses that
most people were familiar with.

LOW MAGIC

Charms & Curses Words of power, these were
intended to bring about the change desired by the
speaker (*see p. 81–82*). Nowadays charms are most evident on bracelets, or as amulets or talismans (*see p. 87*)

that people carry about with them. They can also, of course, be spells – to bring good luck and to protect against bad, even breaking curses if necessary. This was a charm said over a cut to stop it bleeding:

> *In the blood of Adam death was taken,*
> *In the blood of Christ it was all to-shaken,*
> *And by the same blood I do thee charge*
> *That thou do run no longer at large.*

Curses were the opposite, said to bring down evil or bad luck on others. They were believed to be most effective if set at the waning moon or at a new moon. Usually this was done by taking something of the victim's, such as hair or nail clippings (*see pp. 39, 46*), as a medium to send the curse. It was vital that any such cuttings were burned to stop them falling into ill-wishers' hands. Less often, the curse might come via a familiar or some other demonic creature.

Demons & Devils Sometimes summoned by ritual witchcraft but more often simply ill-wishing spirits and agents of the Devil whose sole purpose was to entrap human souls and lead them to damnation. They also explained away any seemingly inexplicable illness or other type of bad luck.

Often, though, it was the Devil himself who went about his own demonic work. Ghosts, fairies, witches and even worshippers of other religions than Christianity were all implicated in some sort of associ-

*The Devil
of popular
imagination*

ation with him.
He could also
possess peo-
ple, as seen in
those prone to
fits, epilepsy
or madness.
Again, any type
of mischief, real
or imaginary,
could be attributed
to him. He was usually
imagined as ugly, as here,
although sometimes he appeared
as a beautiful young man to lure women away.

Medicine As can be inferred from the examples in
this book, this was a type of magic that depended
partly on charms, partly on herbal lore and made no
clear distinction between natural and supernatural
cures. Another important facet, healing by touch, was
something that was even practised by the monarch,
especially for scrofula-sufferers. The practice only died
out three centuries ago; the infant Samuel Johnson

was one of Queen Anne's 'patients'. In the absence of a knowledge of herbalism or any other cure that might be resorted to, healing by touch seemed as good a bet as any.

Wise Women & Cunning Men These were the real medical practitioners and healers but medicine was not their only talent. They were respected in the community and people also turned to them for help with things such as the recovery of lost or stolen items and thief-detection. Their methods included:

- sticking a pair of shears in a sieve and letting those suspected hold the shears; on asking who was guilty, the sieve swung round to point out the culprit

- putting a key into the bible and writing the suspects' names on pieces of paper which were put into the the hollow end of the key; when the culprit's name passed through, the book shook and the key fell out

- rolling up bits of paper bearing the suspects' names and dropping them into a bucket of water; the one that unrolled first was the guilty party

Some wise people used other methods, like astrology or mirrors, to find out the guilty person.

Witches It is evident that in centuries past, belief in witches and their power was almost universal. Not the black-cloaked, broomstick-riding hags of

Hallowe'en imagination, witches were a part of every community. The term could include a wise woman, healer or even an old person living alone with only an animal for company. In many cases, witches might be those with a little more knowledge than their neighbours, objects of jealousy in the neighbourhood and therefore ripe for denunciation, or simply poor deranged souls with over-stoked imaginations who genuinely believed themselves to possess special powers.

The practice of magic was generally held in some awe and suspicion, although the magic itself might be neutral and the intent behind it good or evil. Most witches tended to be seen as good or bad,

A 17th-century witch (flying without the benefit of a broomstick)

although there was still some overlap: a cunning woman who gave someone a charm to triumph over another person, might well be denounced as an evil witch by the vanquished party. Wise women, cunning men and witches were able to co-exist in relative peace with their neighbours and often enjoyed their respect; it was only with the Inquisition on the Continent and the Reformation that the situation got difficult for them.

Fairies

Fairies So many were the types of fairies of popular belief that whole dictionaries have been written to describe them all. Fairies were not necessarily bad, but were never entirely free of suspicion of diabolic association. Some people believed they were spirits who had been thrown out of Heaven with Lucifer, but for a lesser crime that was not bad enough to see them damned to Hell. Like the darker spirits they might be in association with, they were blamed for many misfortunes – from cows that would not milk and butter that would not be churned, through the scale of wickedness to causing strokes, paralysis and abduction.

There were generally thought to be several types of fairy creatures: worker-fairies, who helped humans; fairies who spent all their time making merry and dancing; water fairies; and monsters and giants.

The fairies usually lived in unfrequented, remote places – hills, hollows, caves – and people went near them at their peril. Fairy rings – discoloured rings of grass or flowers where the fairies were believed to dance – were also regarded with dread and given a wide berth. It was believed that someone who walked round such a ring on the night of a full moon would see or hear the fairies. And anyone entering a fairy ring on certain charmed nights, such as Hallowe'en, ran the risk of abduction.

The seductive perils of dallying with the fairies – a dancer is irresistibly drawn into the fairy ring

Fairy theft Fairies were known to covet human children and would steal them if they could, substituting a sickly child of their own in its place. Terrible 'cures', sometimes ending in death, were meted out to the poor innocents suspected of being changelings. It wasn't just babies that were stolen: stroke victims (the full term is 'fairy-stroke') were commonly believed to have been taken by the fairies, and an image that, by magic, seemed like the missing person, left in their place. And anyone unlucky or stupid enough to be in the area of a fairy hill or fairy ring without a suitable protection or repellent was a prime candidate for abduction. Most were kept forever, although a lucky few escaped: the Scottish seer and poet Thomas the Rhymer became the lover of the fairy queen of the Borders' fairy-ridden Eildon Hills. The three days he spent with her in the hills turned out, on his return, to have been three years. Like a latter-day alien abductee, he was ever after at her bidding, obliged to return whenever she called.

House fairies Not all fairies took people away – some actually came to live in humans' houses. These were usually the helpful types, the worker-fairies. The most typical of these was the brownie. These little brown-dressed men worked nightly around the home and farm to complete all the day's work left undone by the servants, expecting only a bowl of cream and a little food to be left out in return.

The other side of this coin was the fairy that minor
annoyances were blamed on. From things spilled or
upset through objects going missing or even just the
milk going off, boggarts (a brownie's mirror-image),
bogies and other pests were held responsible.

Fairy animals Fairies didn't just take human form –
some of the most feared supernatural creatures were
fairy animals. These lived in the wild and wandered
about seeking out their own evil work to do; they
included:

- fairy horses like the kelpie that lived near water; it
  lured the unsuspecting onto its back to carry them
  to a watery grave

- fairy dogs, like the yell hounds (companions of
  Herne the Hunter) or the black dog (see p. 134)

- fairy cattle, less fierce and sometimes benevolent

- fairy sea creatures like the selkie (see p. 144)

Other creatures, like cats and eagles, had strong fairy
associations.

It was bad luck to mention any type of fairy by name
– someone could never tell when they might be listen-
ing and take umbrage. The list on the following page
shows how the fearful and the careful avoided giving
offence.

FAIRY EUPHEMISMS

- the little people
- the good neighbours
- the honest folk
- the hill folk
- the forgetful people
- the men of peace
- the gentry

Foretelling the Future

PREDICTIONS

Omens and prophecies were the life-blood of the superstitious lore that was believed and practised daily, and they were sought in every tiny event. They could include reading the cards (*see p. 110*) or stars (*see p. 121*), or counting out names and numbers (*see pp. 56–57*); more common was to see visions, in dreams (*p. 21*), ghosts and other supernatural warnings. The most common type was the interpretation of everyday events: from the appearance of the early-morning sun, right down to watching how the cows lay in the field, nothing was wasted when it came to superstition and prophesy. In such an uncertain world, people looked for reassurance anywhere and everywhere.

VISIONS
Ghosts

From ghoulies and ghosties,
Long-leggity beasties,
And things that go Bump in the night,
Good Lord deliver us.

(Scottish prayer, c. 1800)

The souls of the dead passed over and come back to haunt the living? Or souls in Purgatory, unable to find rest? Despite the pooh-poohing of Reformation preachers when it came to belief in ghosts, all religious groups and types of people in society believed in their existence. They came back for many reasons, but what they had in common was a desire for vengeance, justice or to right wrongs. A murderer could expect to be haunted; a widow who had broken a promise not to marry again might get a visitation from her first husband; and potential graverobbers or body-snatchers

A red-bound rowan cross: a popular ghost repellent

GHOST REPELLENTS

- make a cross out of two pieces of rowan tree, tie it together with red string or thread and wear it inside your coat

- on meeting a ghost, spit on the ground between you and the ghost and ask it, 'In the Name of the Lord, what do you wish?'

knew a haunting punishment would await them.

Visions Most of the visions that people had were not so dramatic as ghostly visitations. Some extreme believers might be prone to visions of a religious nature, but these were a small minority. Most people who had visions, or claimed they did, had sought them out or brought them on voluntarily. These visions usually came after the performance of a small rite and involved queries about marriage, future husbands and children. This ritual is typical: an unmarried woman who wants to induce a vision of her future husband should pick an ash leaf while chanting:

Even-ash, even-ash, I pluck thee,
This night my own true love to see,
Neither in his rick nor in his rare,
But in the clothes he does everyday wear.

COLLINS GEM
BABIES'
names
a
?
z

a mine of information

COLLINS GEM
BEER

a mine of information

COLLINS GEM
BIRDS

a mine of information

COLLINS GEM
CALORIE
Counter

a mine of information

COLLINS GEM
FACT FILE

a mine of information

COLLINS GEM
FENG SHUI

a mine of information

COLLINS GEM
FLAGS

a mine of information

COLLINS GEM
Healthy
EATING

a mine of information

COLLINS GEM
QUOTATIONS

a mine of information

COLLINS GEM
SAS
Self-Defence

a mine of information

COLLINS GEM
SAS
Survival Guide

a mine of information

COLLINS GEM
SEASHORE

a mine of information

COLLINS GEM
TREES

a mine of information

COLLINS GEM
Understanding
DREAMS

a mine of information

COLLINS GEM
WILD
flowers

a mine of information

COLLINS GEM
WINE
Dictionary

a mine of information